THE 7 ESSENTIAL STRATEGIES FOR PARENTING TEENS

KATE ANDERSON & LIZ CARRINGTON

CONTENTS

A Special Gift to Our Readers

Included with your purchase of this book is our '20 *Simple Tips You Must Use When Talking To Your Teen*' e-book.

This resource will prepare you with the best tools for communicating with your teens effectively and help build more positive relationships with them.

Click the link below or scan the QR code and let us know which email address to deliver it to.

http://eepurl.com/hESnOP

INTRODUCTION - TEENAGERS

If you have one, you'll certainly agree that they're the most complex beings roaming the earth. They go from being our sweet babies to our best friends to our biggest haters — all in the span of ten minutes. And in the face of these confusing, contradictory moods and behaviours, how are we, as parents, supposed to remain loving and calm?

We admit it: we winged parenthood for the first 13 years. We got through alright, until adolescence hit and we became vulnerable. We couldn't just improvise any longer, so we needed some serious tips and tricks to help us raise the well-balanced, empowered young persons we aspire to rear. We started researching and speaking to parents — we couldn't believe all the information out there! We spent over a year sorting through it all, asking other parents endless questions, applying some of the knowledge, and testing what worked best for our families, our teens and our students. Then we compiled it all in this book.

Here, you'll find eight chapters chock-full of the best information and actionable insights we uncovered to help us guide our kids through adolescence. And if these things work for us, we are certain that at least some of them will be valuable to your family as well.

Before all else, it's vital to understand our subject from the inside out. Sure, our teens' bodies are changing, their sex hormones are raging, but it's their brains that play the biggest role in their so-called unruliness.

What does the teenage brain look like? Well, their 'thinking' brain is still under construction at this stage, doing what scientists call synaptic remodeling. They're throwing out bits that aren't useful anymore (like learning how to use a fork) and forming new connections that will serve them for the future. There's some powerful stuff happening in their brains right now, and that can sometimes slow down the rest of their body. (How long does it take your teen to get ready to leave the house?)

Because their cognitive processing won't be fully developed until they're well into their twenties, teens see the world through the emotional part of their brains, the amygdala. We'll dive more deeply into this in Chapter 1, but what this essentially means is that teenagers interact based on feelings rather than thinking or logic. Most adults, on other hand, tend to think too much. We assume everything is logical to everyone, but our teens haven't even begun to see life in that way. That's a valid basis for misunderstandings, don't you think?

Science aside, we'll also look at what our teens really think of us. *Ouch!* This is the right time for us to look back on what *we* were like as teenagers. Taking quiet time to self-reflect is beneficial in all areas of our lives, and can help us put our children's behaviours into context. So, how were you at 15? Between us, we were moody, confused, difficult at times and more concerned about pleasing our friends than anything else. Sound familiar? By thinking back on how we were at their age, it can help us better relate to our own teens.

It's vital to understand the different components of adolescence, but it's just as important to think about how we are as parents. What kind of parent are you? Are you the good cop, or the bad cop?

After doing all this research and speaking to dozens of other parents of teens, it turns out many of us are just as inconsistent as our kids are. We find ourselves going from super disciplinarian to indulgent and uninvolved in the same afternoon. Are you what's called a helicopter parent, someone who hovers over their child to make sure they're always safe, or more of a free-range mom or dad, who lets them function independently to sometimes crash and learn from their own mistakes?

At times couples fall on different ends of the parenting spectrum, and that can cause friction in the home as well. And if you can feel that tension, you can bet your teens feel it too. In Chapter 2, we'll look at what to do when parents disagree.

This book will bring us face-to-face with some hard truths about how our behaviour affects theirs, both positively and negatively. Others are mirrors of ourselves — and our teens, although likely more sporadic, are no different.

That's why we're going to go through seven simple strategies to communicate more effectively, with our teens and in general. You'll learn how to be more observant, a better listener, and how to choose the appropriate language and ask the right questions to get your teens to open up to you. Our goal is for this book to help you develop a stronger relationship based on trust and respect.

We'll also look at the most effortless ways to deal with conflict. (NOTE: Conflict with a teen can stem from anywhere between them borrowing your hairbrush and not returning it to its place to 'borrowing' the car and driving it home over the limit.) Confrontation is always a delicate subject, and in Chapter 5, you'll learn the best ways to have difficult conversations with your kids.

Lazy? Disrespectful? Pushing the boundaries and your buttons, *all the time*? As well as being a rollercoaster of attitudes and emotions, teens are champion negotiators. This book will teach you how to take your own negotiation skills to the next level.

Parenting is heavy-duty work and it's easy to get wrapped up in all the strategies and discipline, in the limits, the logistics and day-to-day necessities. Let's not forget, however, that creating a positive, lighthearted home environment is also part of our role as parents. We all want our teens to feel loved and comfortable, and to actually want to spend time with us. That's why at the end of this book we've included a long list of ideas and projects that you and your teen can do together. We assure you that these activities will pass your teen's 'coolness' test and help build connections for your family as a whole.

And as you go through this book and learn to self-reflect, communicate and negotiate better, don't forget to laugh. Is there anything more joyous than the sound of your children laughing?

The role of a parent is to raise happy, kind, independent humans who can take care of themselves out in the big, sometimes overwhelming world. To do this, we need to set limits and expectations, but also examples of what it's like to be happy and kind humans. We have to show our teens the benefits of being generous, curious and brave so that they, too, are inspired to be so.

If more of us parents apply the strategies in this book, together we can raise a generation of empowered young adults who will go after their dreams and change the world for the better. And for that, we are grateful.

ONE

HOW DOES YOUR TEEN VIEW THE WORLD?

Teenagers are, more often than not, perceived to be bustling beings of complexity. Most parents don't understand why their teens behave so erratically. And that's perfectly normal because even teenagers themselves don't know.

Adolescence is a cocktail of hormones, of physical, emotional, cognitive and social transformations happening simultaneously and working to eventually produce the adult your teen will become.

During this transition from child to adult, teenagers are seeking out their independence while trying to carve out their own identities. They're trying to figure out who they are, what they like, what they're good at, and where they stand in this big, beautiful yet challenging world. Thinking and becoming accountable for themselves is, in fact, what we've been teaching them to do all these years.

But as we know, it isn't as simple as that.

One of our main struggles as parents of teens is finding a balance between the right amount of love and discipline, independence and responsibility. We don't want to smother them, but we certainly don't want to ignore or neglect them either. And it's rare that our kids will tell us the kind of support and attention they want from us. Their developing brains don't know how to assess and communicate those needs yet. To make things even more complicated, finding the right equilibrium as a family varies greatly depending on which stage of adolescence we're dealing with — and on what kind of day we're all having.

All teenagers go through these exciting stages, no matter their social, economic, religious or ethnic background. It's part of growing up, a delicate decade when our kids' brains and bodies are at a critical stage of development.

Other factors like temperament, environment and nutrition influence our teens' maturity, but their changing brains and bodies are behind most of the doubts and debates, power struggles, tears, over-reactions and adaptations that most families go through. These confrontations are inevitable, but after reading this book, you should also be able to add comprehension, connection and laughter to the list that defines these times.

So what drives teenagers? And what's the psychology behind their adolescent transformation?

As parents of teens, we were incredibly curious, so we went out and did the research. In this chapter, you'll get to know adolescents in a more scientific way. Since they're not able to communicate clearly at this stage, our findings will help you better understand your teens and what they're going through.

The Adolescent Brain

The brain reaches its biggest size in early adolescence – but that doesn't mean it has stopped growing. In fact, neuroscientists say our brain is constantly changing throughout our entire lives.

The brain is very complicated to understand as it's the most complex organ of the human body. We've simplified it here and divided it into three main parts.

The Reptilian Brain

The reptilian brain is the part of the brain concerned for our survival. Located at the base of the brain, it acts unconsciously and instinctively, controlling basic and involuntary functions like breathing, body temperature, balance, and gross motor skills. It's highly territorial and seeks pleasure instead of pain. It's in charge of our reproductive needs, so the reptilian brain also controls our primal and sexual instincts – this explains the natural sexual frustration that teens feel as they're trying to understand who they are.

The Limbic System

The limbic system is our emotional hub, and this is where most of the action happens during adolescence. This complex part of the brain is responsible for long-term memory storage and assessment, determining rewards and punishments, and assimilating all kinds of social information.

The main players of the limbic system are the amygdala, hypothalamus and hippocampus. Together, they are very active and yes, *over-reactive* at this stage in life. They process the basic senses like sight, sound and touch, and are the ones that control our impulsive and dramatic reactions. This part of the brain is what incites our teens to think: 'This doesn't sound like a good idea, but I want to do it anyway.'

The limbic system is also responsible for personal motivation, or lack thereof. Ever wonder why those favourite hobbies get stuffed in the back of the closet, or how even the most exciting event fails to get our kids out of bed early? That's thanks to the limbic system.

As parents, it's vital to understand that this rambunctious part of the brain is operating at full force throughout all of adolescence. In the meantime, the logical part of the brain, the cortex, is still under construction.

The Cortex

The cortex is the intellectual part of the brain responsible for complex thinking and skills. Reason, advanced logic, time management, planning, organization, thinking ahead, negotiation, evaluating risks — all of these so-called executive skills take place in the front of the brain, which will only reach maturation once our teens are in their mid-twenties.

(*Did you just have an Ah-ha! moment too?*)

It's no wonder that, as parents of teens, we often ask ourselves:

- Why doesn't she think before she acts?
- Why do I have to tell her ten times?
- Why can't he see the reason or logic in what I'm trying to teach him?

It turns out it's simple: our teenagers' brains just don't work that way — yet.

Their prefrontal cortex is undergoing synaptic pruning, which means the brain is trimming back and eliminating information it no longer uses or needs. Certain synapses, or connections, that were formed as young as two or three years old have gotten weak from disuse, and so they're being discarded to make way for newer, more elaborate neural pathways. It's as if the front part of the adolescent brain is being cleaned up so that more mature executive skills can move in.

The adolescent brain has a lot of neuroplasticity, and while it's undergoing great transformation, it adapts easily and responds to its environment. That's why it's important to create a positive, loving home and structure for our teens. It's also a prime time for them to learn something new, or to start training in a subject or activity they're passionate about.

The Metamorphosis

Much like a butterfly, adolescents are undergoing a process of metamorphosis. Between the ages of 13 and 19, they're at that awkward pupa stage, transitioning from immature to mature and slowly, cautiously, figure out their true colours.

We've just shone the spotlight on their big, beautiful brains, so now let's explore what's happening inside the rest of their cocoons.

On a day-to-day basis, our teens are showing stronger feelings that we, as parents, don't always understand. Their actions and behaviours may appear irrational because when we ask them what's happening, they're not able to clearly describe, or even control, their feelings yet.

Without thinking, our adolescents are tuning into their gut feelings more and sharpening their intuition. They're becoming more perceptive and sensitive to the emotions of others and are attempting to interpret body language and facial expressions. They're sometimes likely to misread our signals, though, and as parents, we need to be patient and accepting of the mistakes they make in judgment.

Being understanding of this transition will help them build their confidence and resilience to bounce back from mistakes and difficult situations.

And we guarantee that there will be plenty of these difficult situations! Our kids are undergoing a great metamorphosis, especially in the early teenage years. Natural chemical reactions and processes related to physical growth lead to a rollercoaster of emotional, cognitive and social changes, too.

Everything in these complex beings is interconnected, and our teens' physical changes also influence their needs, moods and interests. Of course, it is important to note that each child's growth journey will vary slightly.

The Pre-Teen Years

Our children's bodies start changing significantly around the age of ten (give or take a few years), so it's important to talk to them about the physical and emotional changes that are going to happen or are already underway. The more prepared they are for puberty, the less preoccupied or anxious they'll feel when embarrassing body changes occur.

Regarding their bodies, it's always best to be open with our children about what they're going through. As much as they strive for their independence, most teens don't like to stand out from the crowd, so it's reassuring for self-conscious young teens to know they're normal and that everyone else is going through the same changes. Most of their peers will also be curious, questioning their identity and comparing themselves to others.

The early teen years may be some of the most difficult for parents, who have spent the last decade raising a human and forming a bond. All of a sudden, BANG! Your child pushes you away, is no longer receptive to cuddles, starts keeping their door closed and doesn't want to talk.

> *We found this sudden change in our teens quite overwhelming when they started their freshman years. There was a notable increase in the number of home study tasks, social outings with friends, more sports fixtures and events — not to mention their need for more time to themselves, even when at home. Almost overnight, they went from spending a lot of quality time with us every evening and most of the weekends to getting home later on weekdays, having a quick fix dinner then retiring to their rooms for study until bedtime. At first, this transition was hard to accept but after reading and researching the topic, it was clear that this is what they needed to fulfill the aspirations, obligations and interests in their lives.*

This need for more privacy is absolutely normal as our children become more self-aware and start thinking more about themselves. This is often when family conflict will begin, especially when parents don't realize what their young teens are going through. Typically, parents want to spend more time with their growing kids, whilst their kids might want just the opposite.

Their thinking is very black and white at this stage, and younger teens don't quite see the nuances in situations. It is at this point in life when more abstract thinking makes an appearance.

The Mid-Teen Years

This second phase of adolescence usually happens from around 14-17 years old. Once menstruation begins, girls' bodies slowly stabilize, whereas boys tend to find themselves in mid-puberty at this stage.

Very concerned with their bodies and appearances, teens begin to experiment with different images, styles, fashion, music, art. This quest for identity, for who they want to be and who they want others to think they are, is a vital part of growing up. Try not to judge these changes or fashion fauxpas, and if their tendencies are not harming themselves or others, they might even be worth encouraging.

Those in their mid-teens sometimes live in an idealistic, fantasy world. Remember that the emotional parts of their brains are raging at this stage, whereas the more logical part is still in development.

As they feel more confident and comfortable, they become more impulsive and start taking more risks.

> *One of the parents we worked with told us that their daughter had started dating a popular boy at school who was a few years older than her. Sienna admitted to doing this because she had had such a hard time not being liked at elementary school. She went through a transformation in her appearance and style to ensure she was more accepted and likable once she started her freshman year. This worked well for her and Sienna quickly made friends. Her parents told us that she had instigated this whole plan herself and had actually been very responsible about her decision-making so they chose to support her.*

Teens this age are struggling for independence from their families and turning more and more to their friends, looking for the right peer group to identify with. They begin exploring relationships and might venture into more romantic and sexual situations. They're learning to deal with the stress put on them by school, their parents, their peers and other groups. It's often around this time that they are ready to take on more responsibility, like a part-time job or getting themselves from point A to B.

At this stage, teens are able to think more abstractly and see a bigger part of the picture, but as the front of their brains is still undergoing construction, it's difficult for them to think through more complex decisions. By now, they should have a good sense of what's right and wrong, and as parents, we still play a big role in that.

As much as they turn to their friends for short-term decisions, parents remain the main reference for more important long-term decisions and values. They're taking what they've learned from us outside of the home now, comparing it to what their peers and other adults are thinking, and exploring boundaries. The internet, cell phones and social media also play a major role in how they see and interact with the world.

The Late Teen Years

By the time they're 18, most teenagers (now technically young adults) have finished their physical development. They are better able to deal with their impulses and gauge risks and rewards more clearly.

They tend to be more confident in their body image and have a stronger sense of who they are, what they want and believe. Their religious, moral and sexual values are still evolving, and they're willing to step away from their peers and focus on one-on-one relationships, both friendly and romantic.

By their late teens, our children are generally more stable in their ideals and relationships. As they get ready to move away from the family, both emotionally and physically, they're more focused on the future, which is comforting for us as parents. They may reach out to establish a more 'adult' relationship with you – especially if you've created a welcome space for that through the application of the techniques in this book!

Factors That Play Into Personality

As much as the descriptions above apply to most teens, it's important that we make a conscious effort to get to know our sons' and daughters' personalities, as they are all different. It might be worth you considering the following questions: What kind of emotions does your son or daughter show, or not show, when faced with certain situations? What do they feel confident about? What are their fears? What triggers them, and how do they feel about important issues?

Researchers Paul Costa and Robert McCrea developed the Five-Factor Theory, a popular idea that helps classify a person's personality using five major factors. Here they are:

Openness to Experience. Teenagers who gladly welcome new adventures tend to be more curious, imaginative and independent. Those who generally shy away from new experiences are seen as more cautious, practical and pragmatic.

Conscientiousness. Teens who are very conscientious often make calculated decisions and are well-organized. Those who have a lower level of conscientiousness tend to be more spontaneous and flexible, but can also be undependable.

Extraversion. Outgoing adolescents thrive in company and are usually quite assertive, whereas the more introverted tend to prefer being alone.

Agreeableness. Very pleasant teenagers are often compassionate and cooperative, although they may also be seen as naive. Those who are less agreeable are usually more competitive, which can also be perceived as being argumentative.

Neuroticism: This trait determines how susceptible your teen is to their emotions. Someone who is very emotionally stable usually remains calm, whereas less stable teenagers have higher chances of experiencing mood swings, anxiety and depression.

Do you recognize your teen here?

A Dutch study was performed on adolescents aged 12 to 22, and was published in a 2017 issue of the Journal of Personality and Social Psychology. Unlike with adults, who tend to have gained a certain level of stability over time, there are still a lot of question marks when it comes to teenagers. Here is what the observations of the study concluded.

- In younger girls, there's often a dip in emotional stability, though this generally increases again as they approach adulthood.
- Boys tend to be less conscientious and less likely to abide by the rules than girls. Over time, however, both boys and girls were found to increase in conscientiousness, though boys a little bit later than girls.
- Agreeableness, or wanting to please and be liked by others, generally grows with age.
- Teenagers prefer to associate with those who share similarities. When their friends' personalities change, however, instead of changing to become more like them, teens are more likely to discontinue the friendship and seek others to connect with instead.

The Truth About Teens

Now that you understand the different chemical, physical and emotional dimensions of your teen's transformation into adulthood better, you might feel less annoyed, more compassionate and understanding of what they're going through.

But don't get too hopeful yet – they can at times still find us incredibly annoying!

Over the course of our research, we asked many of our students aged between 12-18 as well as our own children what exactly they found most annoying about their parents.

Here, we have collated and outlined the most common issues raised by this collection of youngsters with a brief message suggested by some of the group about how we, as parents, should try to perceive them.

- **"When our parents tell us to act like adults but treat us like kids."**

They're not babies anymore, and although physically they may look like adults, they're not quite yet. Try to find the right balance.

- **"When our parents preach one thing but do the opposite."**

We are their biggest role models, so if we want to teach them values and integrity, we must represent those ourselves.

- **"When our parents don't stop nagging."**

Our teens don't want us to ask questions about every little detail of their lives – they wouldn't answer them anyway. Our children are our biggest observers, and they get especially annoyed when we nag about things we are guilty of doing ourselves.

- **"When our parents don't give us the space and privacy we need."**

Unless you have reason to believe your child is doing something dangerous, trust that they know what they're doing.

- **"When our parents spy on us."**

Be confident that you've raised them well enough — and when you do want to check on them, be transparent about it by letting them know.

- **"When our parents don't realize that we're trying to become independent and don't let us do things for ourselves."**

Although they need your support and guidance, your sons and daughters want to be able to make their own mistakes.

- **"When our parents don't let us express our doubts, confide our fears and explore other options."**

Things are very different from when we were teenagers, so it's not always the best idea to compare their challenges to ours.

- **"When our parents are constantly judging the choices we make."**

Let your teens explore, and be very careful when criticizing their friends. This might make them turn against you.

Now, do you see yourself in any of these complaints? We, too, were guilty of some of these actions, and just being aware of them has transformed us into more conscientious parents. We're going to dive more deeply into self-reflection in Chapter 3, but for now, just knowing what triggers your teen can help you improve your relationship.

Notably, the most shocking point they made was that they think it is naturally their job to push the boundaries. So watch out — but read on to find the best tips on how to deal with this when it happens.

What Teens Really Want From Us

With all those slammed doors and dismissive eye rolls, you'd think that teens would like us to back off and stay out of their lives. I'm sure you've even heard those exact words shouted at you recently.

But no. It turns out that, although they long for independence, all their disdain is only skin-deep. Sure, they tend to take their anger and frustrations out on those closest to them, but unless parents have been noticeably absent or cruel, deep down, most teens really value and respect us.

According to the article, *The Four Truths About What Teens Really Want* published on imom.com, their focus groups and street interviews with teens showed that they don't want 'hands-off parenting'. Teens want us to play our role as parents, to set guidelines and limits. And although they almost always argue and fight against these same limits, they need their parents to provide the wisdom, guidance and discipline that will lead them to become strong, resilient adults.

When we take charge and stick by what we say, teens see it as a form of love and security. In fact, they tend to lose respect for us and discount our authority when we don't enforce the rules. Teens appreciate and respect our rules more when they are justified, so needless to say, it's important to set consistent guidelines and clearly explain the reasons behind them. The teens interviewed also admitted that even 'good kids' need watchful attention and discipline. Remember that the part of the brain that evaluates the pros and cons of actions is not yet fully developed, so even the seemingly most responsible kids need supportive guidance.

What teens don't need is us trying to turn every conversation or incident into a lesson. (*Guilty, again!*) Those constant reminders about what could happen if they start hanging out with the wrong crowd, get tattoos and piercings, don't eat their veggies or don't study enough take away all the fun, making them dread opening up to us. Our teens are more perceptive than we think, so if we've told them once (twice or three times), they don't want to hear these little lessons repeatedly. Sometimes it's important to just listen, laugh and be silly with our kids.

We have to face the fact that we tend to look at our teens from age 12 onward as mini-adults, and that's a mistake we've all made. They're not yet programmed to make the best, most logical decisions – at least not in the way we see it.

This often divergent approach to interacting with the world can lead to a breakdown in communication between parents and teens. If we don't understand why our kids are reacting the way they are, these conflicts can easily spiral out of control. This chapter has highlighted that it's not always their fault. As parents or carers, we need to seriously think about the way in which we react to our sons and daughters.

That's why we've given you a sneak peek into what annoys our kids, and what they expect from us as parents. And now that we know that all teens are emotional and impulsive – it's not just ours! – we can accept that truth and use the techniques outlined in this book to improve our relationships and become more confident, stress-free parents.

TWO

WHAT ARE YOUR PARENTING STYLES?

There are as many types of parents as there are teenagers, and we continue to grow and evolve along with them. It's a time of transition, and what may have worked for you in your child's earlier stages of development might no longer be the best approach. In this chapter, you will learn about the myriad of parenting approaches used around the world — and you will most certainly recognize yourself in one or more of them.

As we were researching the different styles of parenting, we noticed that most of the parents we had discussions with did not fit into one single category. We tend to be a combination of the styles we'll look at below. Sometimes we're too permissive, other times overly controlling. We want to give our kids everything we can, but we're also afraid of spoiling them, which may sometimes lead to neglect. We have found that we move between the different parenting styles depending on the behaviour our children display, what stage they are at, how many deadlines we have looming as well as countless other factors.

No parent is perfect. If you are struggling to cope with your teen, do not label yourself a 'bad parent' or decide that you have a 'bad kid'. You are simply a parent looking to find better ways to understand and deal with the issues you are having with your teen. And just the fact that you're reading this book means you're making an effort and are on the right path.

Building a solid relationship with our sons and daughters is not only about adapting to their needs and the different situations that arise with each age group. It's also about being a conscious parent.

What Is Conscious Parenting?

Conscious parenting is about focusing on what we need as adults and becoming more mindful. (We will discuss this concept in greater detail in Chapter 3.) But in essence, being a conscious parent is about looking inside ourselves, to our own past and personal experiences, and realizing that we don't need to constantly weigh our kids down with our baggage. Our sons and daughters are independent beings, and as conscious parents we try to truly understand how they think, what they need and what is behind their behaviours. By the time they've reached adolescence, chances are we've realized that our kids won't become exactly who we had planned, expected or hoped they would. And that's perfectly fine.

Practicing mindfulness, acceptance and tolerance for both ourselves and our children helps build a stronger bond. Mindful parenting is often a long, challenging process, and self-reflection is a vital tool in becoming a (more) conscious parent. We'll provide some valuable exercises on how to get the most out of self-reflection in the next chapter.

In the meantime, don't feel bad about yourself if you make a parenting mistake — we all make them! Some emotions, words or behaviours trigger certain reactions in us, and these reactions are not necessarily what's best for our family. Like our children, we, too, are continuously growing and should reflect on how we interact with our kids, as opposed to allowing ourselves to be provoked and reacting how we're accustomed to. Instead of trying to take control of everything around you, show your teens that it's okay to fail, as long as you try to improve next time. Push yourself outside of your comfort zone for the sake of a healthier, more communicative and stress-free relationship. Inspire your teens to also do this for themselves.

The Four Classic Parenting Styles

While becoming a conscious parent is an aspiration, most of us are currently operating with a variety of other parenting styles. Your parenting style refers to the combination of strategies you use to raise your children, and the way we raise our kids will likely have an impact on their future romantic, peer and parenting relationships. That's why it's important to think about what's working and what's not working in the different stages of your child's life.

Many psychological studies have been done to define the different styles. One of the most widely referenced is the work of clinical and developmental psychologist Diana

Baumrind. In the 1960s, her research with preschool-aged children revealed three distinct types of parenting: authoritative, authoritarian and permissive. She analyses these based on how responsive we are towards our children's needs as well as how demanding we are of them. Other parenting styles were later added to the list, and we'll look at these too.

It's eye-opening to reflect on where you fall within the parenting spectrum. You do not have to assign yourself to just one style, as you'll probably see yourself falling into different styles at different times. As a parent it's up to you, however, to learn what each type of parenting entails, and how you can adapt your style to improve your relationship with your teen.

Authoritative Parenting

This is the most balanced form of parenting. Authoritative moms and dads are characterized by reasonable demands and high responsiveness to their children's needs. This means they are consistently warm and loving, have high expectations of their kids and use fair discipline and positive reinforcement. Rules are set and expected to be obeyed (as all our rules should be!), but the family runs in a wholehearted, democratic way. Rules and boundaries are openly discussed and negotiated, and teens' opinions are taken into account.

Authoritative parenting is a child-centric approach that helps build children's independence. Our sons and daughters will not always do what we expect of them, and that's normal. Those who practice this parenting style are more likely to understand and forgive their teen's weaknesses, and be strong, positive influences for them when they stray off course. These types of parents offer the support and guidance needed to teach their kids how to behave in the future.

According to Baumrind, authoritative parents "...are assertive, but not intrusive and restrictive. Their disciplinary methods are supportive, rather than punitive. They want their children to be assertive as well as socially responsible, and self-regulated as well as cooperative."

Over the years, studies have shown that children with authoritative parents are most likely to become comfortable, responsible adults with solid decision-making skills. They tend to be happy and successful in life.

As much as possible, we aim to remain within this style of parenting as it helps us ensure that the household runs smoothly.

Authoritarian Parenting

This type of parenting, also known as disciplinarian, sets high demands and expectations on children. They are expected to behave well at all times, and strict punishments are given when they fall out of place. Authoritarian parents are not usually very nurturing or responsive to their children's needs and tend to use a lot of psychological control, often through shaming or withdrawal of love.

If you've ever found yourself telling your child to do something 'just because I said so,' that was the authoritarian in you. This type of parenting offers very little room for negotiation and flexibility, and focuses on obedience and status. Authoritarian parents are demanding, domineering and dictatorial.

Because their opinions aren't valued, children of authoritarian parents are more likely to become hostile and aggressive, and can develop self-esteem issues. Instead of thinking about how to improve in the future, they are often resentful and focus on the anger they feel towards their parents. They may even grow up to become good liars, having had to lie in an effort to avoid punishment.

Expecting children to obey without question is not conducive to closeness, trust and open communication. So when teens feel it's their duty to push the boundaries, as we learned from them in Chapter 1, authoritarian parenting does not seem like the best way to promote a stress-free relationship with your son or daughter. In fact, it feels more like a boot camp than a harmonious family environment.

Permissive Parenting

Also known as indulgent parenting, this style focuses on children's freedom rather than responsibility. As far as Baumrind's studies show, permissive parents are more responsive than demanding, and have low expectations of their child's maturity and self-control. Because of this, they set weak guidelines, provide little discipline, and enforce few consequences to undesirable actions. 'Kids will be kids,' so they say.

Permissive parents are very loving and nurturing, and acutely responsive to their children's emotional needs. They involve kids in major decisions, and may even bribe them to get them to behave. They're lenient, often overly relaxed, and can sometimes be seen as pushovers. They rarely say no.

Permissive folks might seem like the cool parent to some, the ones who let things slide. To avoid confrontation, they would rather let their teens figure things out for themselves. And although they might behave more like a friend than a parent, the adolescents we spoke to in Chapter 1 admitted that they preferred clear family structure and guidelines to be enforced. Teens expect parents to act like parents.

Those who grow up in a permissive household tend to have difficulty making sound decisions and setting their own limits. Used to getting what they want, they may also exhibit poor social skills and be demanding of others. Sadness and insecurity are often bi-products of not having had a clear structure growing up, and kids of permissive parents are more likely to struggle academically, become delinquents and make unhealthy life decisions. Child development experts recognize that permissive parenting is one of the worst parenting styles for raising healthy, responsible adults.

Uninvolved Parenting

Uninvolved parenting was added to Baumrind's list by other researchers in the 1980s. This style offers children lots of freedom, though sometimes to such an extent that it leads to neglect. Uninvolved mothers and fathers may provide the basic needs such as food, shelter and clothing, but often fall short on affection, guidance and connection. They are neither very responsive nor demanding, the two factors that Baumrind established as important for creating well-balanced children. Uninvolved parents expect kids to raise themselves.

Those who function in this style of parenting rarely interact with their children. They tend to be emotionally distant and indifferent about what their child is up to, which can give the impression that they don't care about them. Often, they just don't know any better and are lacking information on how to be a present parent.

Whether they are overworked, have mental health issues or grew up in an uninvolved family environment themselves, neglectful parents do not necessarily realize that they are ignoring and hurting their children. Being wrapped up in their own lives, they may skip important events in their teen's development, leaving their kids to feel unworthy and insecure. Low self-esteem, poor performance and behavioural issues are prevalent in those growing up with uninvolved parents.

We all have moments when we are too busy or ignore our teens, and that's normal. Issues arise when this lack of involvement becomes a pattern. If you recognize yourself in this parenting style, read on. This book is filled with valuable information on how to build a stronger connection with your teen.

Three More Modern Parenting Styles

As times change, it's only normal that so do our parenting strategies. Studies evolve and become more sophisticated, and technology plays a greater role in our everyday lives. While we continue to want what's best for our teens, we're in constant transformation, so here are three different ways that parenting styles have been characterized in more recent years. Can you see yourself in any of these?

Helicopter Parenting

You guessed it! These types of parents hover over their children like a helicopter. They're overly focused on their kids, trying to protect them and clinging onto their plans and expectations of how things should be. Psychologist and author Ann Dunnewold refers to this type of parenting style as overcontrolling, overprotecting, overperfecting.

This style seems to be even more popular with parents of teens, who try to control their soon-to-be adult child's future. They feel overly responsible for their successes and failures, and tend to do things for their sons and daughters that they could easily do themselves — or should have learned how to do by now, if they'd been given more freedom.

Studies have shown that helicopter parenting often stems from feelings of overcompensation, guilt, anxiety and the fear of their kids experiencing negative consequences. Struggles like uncertainty, disappointment, loss and failure, however, are essential in learning how to cope and become more resilient and independent. How else would we learn to deal with everything life throws at us?

By being overprotected, teens of helicopter parents may also feel a certain sense of entitlement, increased anxiety and low self-confidence from feeling that their parents don't trust them. For a healthy parent-teen bond, however, it's vital to let our teens know that we believe in them and that we're there for them whenever they need us.

Attachment Parenting

This style is often connected to early childhood, when parents want to spend as much time as possible physically holding their babies and developing that nurturing connection through breastfeeding and cosleeping.

A strong bond is formed through this unconditional love and emotional support, which reassures children that their parents are there for them. Those who parent in this style practice positive discipline, consistent structure and guidance so that kids learn how to discipline themselves.

Attachment parenting is focused on nurturing your child, not controlling them. It lets them unfold as they are, not as we'd like them to be.

When it comes to teens, attached parents understand and support the ongoing metamorphosis, and promote healthy connections and open communication. These types of parents take the time to listen and get excited about their children's stories and adventures, providing guidance without judgment. Being open to discussing everything, including puberty, sex, philosophy, social justice and their evolving moral principles helps build trust and confidence. This style of parenting deals with children's development holistically and has shown to produce secure, well-balanced, empathetic adolescents.

Free-Range Parenting

Did your mind jump to free-range chickens too? It's a reasonable analogy, as free-range parents allow their children to explore outside freely, with limited parental supervision.

Unlike overly permissive or uninvolved parents, free-range parents make sure their children are good and ready for the real world before sending them out there. Kids have proven to their relaxed parents that they can be responsible and independent, and that they have the skills required to make it home safely. They've earned their increased freedom and responsibility and are raised to be street smart.

This mindset is the opposite of helicopter parenting. While overprotective moms and dads tend to parent out of fear, those who practice free-range parenting trust their children and the universe. By sending their kids outside, they understand that children need to get hurt, face obstacles and learn from their mistakes in order to grow. This freedom teaches self-sufficiency and how to deal with conflict, both of which are invaluable skills for the future.

This liberal stance has been criticized by many, however, as being too risky. How old should kids be before being allowed to walk the streets by themselves or stay home alone? The debate is a fiery one, and there is no right answer. While some view free-range parenting as negligent and downright dangerous, others see it as the opportunity to teach the autonomy and decision-making skills needed to become empowered adults.

Once again, balance and common sense are key. Let your teen have time for unscheduled activities, and send them outside (without their electronic devices!) to explore in nature. What they can learn from that is priceless.

Conflicting Parenting Styles

While reading through the seven parenting styles, you've undoubtedly seen yourself and your co-parent described in one, or several of these categories. We're all unique, and as we grow with our children and try to navigate the stages of parenthood, we embody different parenting traits.

It becomes difficult, however, when we don't agree with the other parent — and this is very common. The main reason for this is because of our own upbringing; inevitably, our own parents adopted certain parenting styles to rear us, same with their parents before that. Parenting is an area where many couples struggle, and we've found this to be especially true during the complex adolescent years. Raising teenagers is far from easy, and it's normal to have conflicting ideas on what's best for our not-so-little ones. There's no doubt we all love our kids, but when it comes to discipline, what should we do when we clash?

Communication Is Key

If you don't have a solid parenting strategy yet, it is fine because we use different approaches at different times. Now, it's time to start thinking about how you might use certain strategies for different purposes. Start with reflecting on how your parents were with you. How were you raised? What do you think is reasonable for your child at this stage in their life? What do you want for your teen in the long run? What do you and your partner agree on? Highlight what you think are your partner's best parenting qualities, and focus on those.

This is a fresh start for you as united parents, so begin on common ground. Think of all the issues you and your teen are going through and make a list. What are your beliefs around education? Bedtime? Freedom? And why? A lot of these beliefs come from our own parents — we've adopted their way of disciplining without even realizing or questioning it. We have often found ourselves thinking, 'Oh wow, we've turned into our mothers...' And you?

Parents may have differing ideas on what their teens should be allowed to do and their level of responsibility, but remember that you're a team. As parents, you're the household leaders, so it's important to stick together and back each other up whenever possible.

Take the time to negotiate and finally decide on specific rules, then agree on fair consequences for stepping out of bounds. And yes, chances are you'll have to compromise. Don't take things too personally and always keep your focus top of mind: you're both doing what's best for your teen. Think about the values you want to instill in your children and work towards those.

Stick to Your Plan

Write down your (new) family guidelines and make sure they're clear for everyone. Then stick to this plan. It's vital for both parents to lovingly reinforce the rules and consequences, otherwise teens may try to manipulate situations. And if you've disagreed on parenting techniques before, you'll know that these discrepancies often lead to family conflict.

Try not to disagree or argue in front of your child. Support one another in your decisions — or at least pretend to in the presence of your kids! Don't undermine the other parent openly, and sort out any problems with your partner in private. A lot of parents blame and resent the other, but remember that we all make mistakes, and parenting is no different.

There tends to be less friction in the home when both parents practice the same style, yet research shows that having at least one authoritative parent is better for the child than having both mom and dad with the same, less effective style. It's all about finding harmony and the right balance.

We can only do our best with the knowledge and tools that we have. Sometimes we employ different styles of parenting with different children, and what may work for one does not necessarily work for the other. Let's not forget that other factors like a child's temperament, teachers and peer group also play a role in your teen's development. Showing your teen unconditional love and respect is one of the most important things you can do.

Try to think about your parenting style objectively, without any self-judgment, and begin to make the changes you feel are right for you and your teen. Be more aware of how you react to situations that trigger you, and work towards becoming a more conscious parent. This will become easier once we look at the next chapter on self-reflection.

REFLECTING ON THE PAST FOR A BETTER FUTURE

L ooking back on our past helps us create a better future.

Self-reflection has been proven to have numerous benefits, like increased awareness of ourselves, our journey and our progress. It encourages acceptance, forgiveness and compassion, and is a valuable tool to use at any moment in life — including when you're in the midst of a whirlwind with your teen.

Thinking back to our own adolescence can help us understand our teens better and see where some of our parenting values and triggers come from.

For example, as a teen you might have felt like you were not truly seen, heard, understood or even appreciated. Often these feelings can manifest into negative thoughts and behaviours as you become an adult. Maybe your parents criticized and yelled at you without trying to fully understand you, and without any thought or knowledge of how teens develop cognitively. Maybe you were not given enough verbal praise for positive behaviour. The way they treated you affects how you treat your own children.

On a personal note, Liz remembers her mother trying to teach her independence by insisting she helps out with chores around the house. She also recalls her father being overly strict about safety on the roads during their driving lessons. She did not feel unloved by these actions, but she did feel hard done by and frustrated, especially since some of her friends got away with not having to do chores. Interestingly, however, today Liz adopts the same approach her parents used by ensuring her teens are more aware of helping around the house — but the difference is they get more recognition for doing so through payment or verbal praise. This ensures they do not feel quite so bad about doing chores.

Reflecting back on our own youth isn't a critique of our parents, but rather a way to comprehend where we come from. Most parents do not want this spiral of unproductive events and experiences for their teens. We want them to feel loved, respected, appreciated and heard.

In this chapter, we'll explore three progressive ways to use reflection, empathy, responsibility, wisdom and experience to ensure that we're in the right mindset to support our teens.

But first, we have to raise ourselves.

Raising Ourselves Before We Raise Our Children

Before we can look after someone else, we must first look after ourselves. Too often, parents get wrapped up, trying to juggle everything around them: family, work, school, hobbies, life. Our own wellbeing gets pushed off to the side-lines, and, slowly or not, depending on our resilience, internal chaos ensues. In this environment, how can we expect our teenagers to feel calm and consistent? It is vital to respect our own physical, emotional and spiritual needs before meeting those of our family.

The advantage we have over our children is that we have been through experiences before them. Beyond that, we are still learning how to deal with growing adolescents and their problems and needs.

Parenting teens should not be viewed as a burden but as a privilege, so it is important not to abuse that privilege. Respect it instead. The aim is to protect our children from improper influences of any sort, and that includes ourselves. We unexpectedly influence our child's choices; that's when self-reflection comes in.

We are our teens' most direct and influential role models, and whether we like it or not, they're taking in everything we do. That's why it's essential to handle life with a positive mindset. Much of their behaviour is based on what they observe from us, be that good or bad, which is a great incentive for us to make the right choices ourselves. It is important to follow our own rules and model the life skills we want our teen to adopt, such as developing healthy habits and respecting others. The way we react to stress, fear and disappointment will likely be the way they'll respond, too. We will explain why our actions matter in more detail in Chapter 4.

So how exactly do we take one step closer to becoming that great role model our teens need? We can begin by diving into the past.

Step 1: Thinking Back to Your Teen Years

According to research, the first seven years of our lives are spent observing everything around us, taking in all sorts of information about how the world works. As teenagers, we've accumulated all this information and are trying to figure out where we fit into this world. Our observations and the feelings connected to them become the frameworks of how we view the world as adults.

This is why taking the time to look back to when we were younger gives us a better understanding of why we are who we are today. We all have childhood wounds that need to be nurtured. Even those of us who were lucky enough to have so-called ideal childhoods have issues that need clearing up.

Thinking back to, untangling and making sense of these events brings us one step closer to making sure we don't repeat these negative patterns with our own children.

Now, carve out some uninterrupted time in your busy life as a teenager's mom or dad. Find a quiet, comfortable place where you won't be disturbed. You may even want to tell your teens what you're doing, so they begin to understand the value of contemplation. If you like, grab a notepad and pen to take some simple notes. What will follow are a series of questions which you can think about. Do not feel overwhelmed by these, and don't spend very much time dwelling on the answers — they are there to simply guide your thinking.

Self-reflection does not need to be a long and tiresome process, yet it has such enormous benefits to the way we think and behave towards our kids. Write your memories and reflections down in quick note form so you can refer to them more easily — chances are you won't be able to integrate everything that comes up for you instantly, so it's a good idea to have notes. In making these notes you will have very productively self-reflected on yourself.

Looking at who we are, why we are that way, and what challenges we continuously face as adults makes us better equipped to raise well-balanced teens.

As part of our research, we advised parents to do the following activity when starting out on their journey to better parenting. The feedback was tremendously positive and parents found two main benefits in going through this process of self-reflection.

Firstly, they explained how thinking about things they would never have normally thought mattered when raising their teen was incredibly useful.

Secondly, the majority of parents who did this exercise noted that they immediately found a connection between their own past experiences and how they were currently raising their children. This was because the questions actually made them contemplate on how they were parenting.

Eight Points for Reflection

You as a teen. What was your personality like? What did you look like? How did your tastes in fashion, music or finding the right friends and partners evolve over the years? Were you confident or shy? In which types of circumstances did you feel most comfortable?

What were your chores and responsibilities around the house? What kind of memories do these bring back? What was school like for you? What do you remember most about your education?

What were your dreams and aspirations? What did you feel inside that you didn't want to share with anyone?

Family. How was your relationship with your parents, siblings and other relatives? How involved were your parents? Did you feel supported by them? Are there ways now in which you try to be like them, or try not to be like them?

Were they curious about your passions, encouraging you to speak your truth, or were you pushed towards things you didn't particularly like? Were you able to communicate freely about how you felt?

What was your relationship with your extended family? Did you see them often? Were you close? Was your home welcoming to friends and family, or did things run on a 'by appointment only' basis?

What did discipline look like for you? What was the general mood in the home? Was it a warm, nurturing environment where you could be yourself, or did you have to watch what you do? The general vibe in your childhood home is often indicative of how grounded you feel as an adult.

Peers and other influences. Did you make friends easily? Did you have many friends, or a small, close-knit group? Where did you and your friends hang out? How long did your friendships last? Why did they end? Do you still have some of those same friends today? Did you have a boyfriend or girlfriend? Were there any other adults, outside of your family, who had a great influence on you?

Values and traditions. What values and principles did you grow up with, and keep? Did your family pass on any stereotypes that you still hold onto today? Did you celebrate certain cultural traditions? Do you know about your culture and your extended family tree? Knowing our roots helps us build connections and understand our past.

Major events and traumas. What were the major events of your childhood? What were the most difficult things about growing up? Did you experience any traumatic events? Did you lose someone close to you? How did these things make you feel then? How do they make you feel today? If you're still holding on to these memories, they can have a big impact on you as an adult.

Hobbies, pastimes and freedom. Were there phone and social media influences when you were a teen? Did you have gaming devices? What did you do to fill your time? What activities did you enjoy, and not enjoy? Did you and your family have any common hobbies or pastimes? What did you do with your friends?

How much freedom did you have in your neighbourhood? Were you allowed to go out to parties or hang around in the parks with your friends? Were you encouraged to do so? Is there anything you would have liked to do but didn't? Why? Did you travel a lot? These types of experiences help develop identity and self-esteem.

Food. What kind of eater were you as a teen? Did your parents emphasize healthy eating habits? Did you ever prepare food for yourself? For your family? Did your family eat meals together? What emotions does food evoke for you now?

Finances. What was the energy surrounding money in your home? Were your parents stressed about finances? Did they budget or spend freely? What did they teach you about money? Did you get an allowance or money as a teen? Did you have to work for it? Our parents' beliefs about money often impact how we manage our finances and view money as adults.

> *Looking back at our own adolescent years, we know that our parents worked hard for their money. We looked forward to treats and knew that we, too, would have to work hard in order to deserve the things we wanted. Our generation was taught to value money, to be savvy and only spend on what was essential at the time. Now we find ourselves educating our own teens to have similar attitudes regarding money.*

Putting Our Past to Good Use

Reflecting on our adolescence is bound to bring up many emotions we haven't necessarily felt or thought of since, well, adolescence. As a way of putting to use all of the memories we've brought back to the foreground, here's another exercise that may help to tie everything in.

First, write a list of the people, memories and values that were a positive influence for you as a teenager. If they were valuable and felt good for you, maybe you'd like to maintain these, or adaptations of these, with your own son or daughter. Implement or continue with meaningful traditions, and instill habits that make sense for both you and your family.

Next, write a list of the people, values and traditions with which you no longer feel a connection. These are the memories from adolescence you do not wish to repeat with your own child, but that you may, in fact, be doing so unknowingly. Try to free yourself of these by re-creating and feeling the emotions attached to the people, values or memories. Tell yourself that you are letting go of these parts of your past, and visualize them floating away from you.

This intentional approach is something we have used and recommended to the parents we worked with. Because you are forced to be conscious about the way you think, it has proven to help release stored negative energy that has been blocking us from becoming our best selves.

Step 2: You as a Parent, Today

Hopefully reflecting back on your adolescence has helped you come to some conclusions about why you are the way you are. Be honest with yourself, non-judgmental, and feel proud that, by reading this book and applying its techniques, you are trying to rectify and create a more harmonious present and future for your family.

But your journey of self-reflection is not over yet! There are still many questions to ask yourself about your current patterns and behaviours. For example, are you the kind of parent who wants to live your dreams through your child? Are you the parent who is overprotective because of the mistakes you made in life? Do you feel you had a terrible adolescence, and that's why you are now too lenient with your teen and are being constantly walked over?

In order to parent consciously, it's important to really think about what kind of parent you are.

- What impact do you think your adolescence has had on your adult life in general? Focus on the ways you see yourself today, and more specifically, on how you relate to your teens.
- How do you think your past experiences have influenced your relationships as an adult? Do you have patterns of behaviour that you'd like to change but are having difficulty changing? What are they?
- If you could change anything about your childhood, what would it be?
- What are your strengths? Your weaknesses?
- How do you cope with life's challenges? Think of your healthy coping strategies as well as the unhealthy ways you deal with stress and struggles.
- Think back to a difficult experience from your childhood. If you could go back in time, what would you want your younger self to know? Now close your eyes, picture yourself at that age and give yourself the support you wish you'd had.

- Where do you feel you are falling short as a parent? Accept this part of yourself with self-compassion and forgiveness.
- Finally, what kind of parent do you want to be?

Now, based on what you've learned about teenagers and the different parenting styles, and including any revelations resulting from your self-reflection, make a plan for your own personal growth. Encourage yourself to become a better, more conscious parent and, as part of your daily routine, give yourself a gentle reminder to put your plans into place.

Why Our Actions Matter

You are your teen's greatest role model. While their friends tend to influence their day-to-day decisions, like the clothes they wear or the music they listen to, we, as parents, play a powerful role in their basic behaviours, attitudes and beliefs. Teens are very quick to imitate others, as they're still searching for their identity, and they often use this as an excuse for their behaviour when questioned.

Our children value our opinions and support, and how we act shows our teens how we want them to behave. How you cope with your feelings, regulate your emotions and take care of yourself all inspire how your teen reacts now and the choices they'll make in the future. What you say also plays a big role, so it's important to communicate openly about emotions, about what's right and wrong and how our behaviours affect others, both positively and negatively.

It bears repeating that none of us are perfect. Sometimes our behaviour is less than commendable, and that also influences our teens. It helps if we're aware of this, so be completely honest now: How often do you act like a child yourself? Are you sometimes untidy, lazy, disorganized? When was the last time you swore, lied, argued or were downright despicable in front of your teen? Do you preach one thing but do the other? Do you break the family rules?

That's okay, and acknowledging weaknesses is a solid step in the right direction. If our teens see us trying to improve on our downfalls, it will reassure them about their own weaknesses and uncertainties. It will teach them that life is a long learning journey and that progress is possible.

In our teaching environment, we strive to ensure we are great role models for our students in the way we speak, listen, dress, react to situations, learn and solve problems. Even our food choices are important. We are aware of how easily adolescents are influenced and how quickly they begin to imitate others, so we have to ensure we are setting a positive example.

While this chapter is about deep introspection, sometimes it's vital to bring ourselves back to the basics — and this is true not just in parenting, but in all aspects of life.

Values like kindness, respect, service and positivity raise our energy and the energies of those around us. They make us better people, and better parents. Here are three points to strive for to enrich your family environment.

Maintain respectful relationships and bound-aries. How you talk to yourself and others sets the example for your children to follow. Be mindful of your words and tone of voice. Do what you say you're going to do and try to respond to challenges calmly.

Make sure to behave in the same way that you would like your teens to behave — or better. It's unfair to ask them to do anything that you, yourself, don't do.

Teach your teens how to set and respect limits. Boundaries are crucial to determining what you, as a parent, needs, as well as what your teens are and aren't allowed to do. Don't take on your teen's problems — they are theirs and an opportunity for a valuable learning experience. Always be there for your teens if they need you, but it's important to let them clean up their own messes, much as you're trying to clean up your own.

Encourage a healthy lifestyle and attitude. Do this for yourself as well as for your children. Pay attention to your habits, including eating, exercise, alcohol consumption, and any addictions you may have. If our teens see us binging on junk food or attached to our mobile phones 24/7, how can we expect them to be any different?

Practice positive self-talk and recognize that you and others are simply doing the best you can. To encourage collaboration and accountability, include your teen in family discussions and show them that you respect and value their input by making sure their voice is heard and part of family decisions.

Notice the good things your kids are doing, not just the bad, and congratulate them (and yourself!) for their actions. What's more, it's important to (re)connect with your partner. Demonstrate affection and appreciation — not only will this strengthen and even rekindle your relationship, it also sets a good example for what a loving family environment should look like.

And as much as your teens need time alone, so do you. Show them that self-care is a vital part of life.

Promote a growth mindset. Being curious about life keeps things exciting, and we're able to learn or improve anything we really put our minds to. Instill your kids with this growth mindset and it will enhance their learning and desire for self-improvement. Likewise, don't be afraid to admit you're wrong or don't know something.

By the time our children are teens, they're able to take on some of the household responsibilities. Not only will this free up some time for you, but making them contribute to family life teaches them skills and maturity for the future. Don't be afraid to ask for support and create a network around you. This relieves some of the pressure and incites teens to connect with other adults and experience different opinions.

Finally, make efforts to change your own attitudes in order to fit into today's modern world. Things are very different from when you were a teen, and being open to learning about what our modern teens are going through will help strengthen that parent-teen bond.

Step 3: Become the Unconditional Provider

Now that you have a deeper understanding of your past and the reasons behind who you are today, you are better equipped to become the unconditional provider every teen needs.

Your old, unconscious habits and triggers are interwoven with your family past and how you were brought up. It isn't until you've dug into your childhood and relived all the experiences and emotions associated with it that you'll be able to remove the blocks that prevent you from parenting unconditionally.

What Is Unconditional Parenting?

It's about providing that absolute love that every child, every human, needs.

Those who are conscious of the significance of unconditional love make the effort to build a parent-teen relationship that is based on tolerance, understanding and cooperation. How you interact with the world is an indication of how your child, too, will interact with the world. Be aware of how your choices, decisions and attitudes will affect your teen.

A simple way to do this is by asking yourself: 'If that comment I just made to my child had been made to me — or if what I just did had been done to me — would I feel unconditionally loved?'

As we know, it's easy to get wrapped up in life and forget our primary purpose as a parent, which is to show love and support while providing shelter and unconditional love. These are every child's basic human rights, so make a clear, intentional decision never to make your own child feel like they are a burden to you.

Acknowledge your teen as the individual you brought into this world.

> *Kate spent some time reflecting back to when she first found out she was expecting a baby. She remembered all the excitement and anticipation involved, and recalled doting on her firstborn, nourishing and caring for him through every situation. She taught him how to talk, read and*

ride a bicycle. Now, she makes a huge effort to remind herself that her 17-year-old son, the one who needs to be reminded about boundaries and comes with a lot of problems and commotion, along with all the other typical teenage issues, is still that same child she nurtured many years ago. She reminds herself that he needs her as much now as he did back then, although in different ways.

Take the time to connect with these memories before jumping to conclusions or making decisions based on triggered reactions, fear, frustration or anger. Don't seek to control your teen. Seek to understand them.

You've hopefully cleared up some blocks and uncertainties from all this delving into your own adolescence and looking back at the years before your child grew so quickly into a teen.

Through research and experience, we've learned that often, it's easier for parents to change the way they think and behave than it is to try to change their teenagers. And self-improvement should always be one of our goals. You will find that once you transform the way you respond to things, the attitudes and relationships at home will also begin to shift in the right direction.

. . .

In the next chapter, we'll explore different approaches to help improve communication with your teen, always keeping in mind the values of conscious and unconditional parenting.

FOUR

SIMPLE STRATEGIES TO COMMUNICATE MORE EFFECTIVELY WITH YOUR TEEN

Communication is an art form. We all know how to speak and listen, but do we *really* know how to do those things? It turns out many of us don't, which is why so many of our problems exist.

Communicating with teens tends to be a great challenge for many parents. At this age, it's normal for our sweet sons and daughters to test our limits and resist authority. By exploring beyond their familiar boundaries, they move away from us — not because they no longer love or need us, but because their world is growing and they're seeking out and building their independence.

As we saw in Chapter 1, the adolescent brain is now developed enough to start grasping more abstract concepts, and our teens are starting to think about moral issues. They're expanding their mental capacities to include more futuristic and philosophical concerns, and have a focus on relationship building.

They're trying to evaluate who they are, what they'll be like in the future, and how to apply what they've learned so far to become their best selves. These normal evolutionary transitions shape and change the way they think and communicate, and that means that we, too, need to adapt.

When you are able to communicate effectively with your teen, they will react and engage effectively in return. This includes body language as well as the word choices and tones we use when speaking.

There's no doubt that parents would like their teens to come to them for guidance and support. We all want to be the voice in their heads that helps them maintain good judgment and stay safe, and in order for this to happen, we have to be the kind of parent they want to share their experiences with.

Let's look at some tried and tested communication strategies that will help you become that type of parent — the one your teenager turns to.

Change the Way You Listen

This is a common mistake: We think we know what our kids are going to say and we interrupt them before they can even finish their thoughts. Now, nobody likes being cut off mid-sentence — especially not our sensitive teens! This makes them feel unheard and disrespected, like we think their words and ideas are 'old news'. If they feel they're not worth listening to, eventually they'll stop sharing with us. And that's the last thing we want as a parent.

We want to build the habit of listening to understand, rather than listening with the intent to respond. Here's how to do that.

Be fully present. We're all busy, but nothing is more important than your teen wanting to open up and share something with you. When they come to you to chat, give them your full attention. Stop what you're doing, put down your phone, and focus on them.

Try to see things from their perspective. Many of their situations and events may seem trivial and over-dramatic to you, but keep in mind that, for our sons and daughters, these things are often happening for the first time. Your teen's world is smaller than yours, their ideas more naive and their emotions more explosive. Attempt to tone down your analytical adult mind and listen to them on their level. Put yourself in your teen's shoes when they're talking to you, and try to remember what it was like to be their age. Reflect their emotions. Don't be afraid to let your feelings show on your face — this lets them know that you're paying attention and can understand, or at least empathize, with how they feel.

Rephrase and repeat what they say. By restating their words, it helps you to really comprehend the different elements of their situation. It shows your child that you're paying attention while also giving them a chance to explain things again if you happen to reword their thoughts incorrectly. This type of interaction is a wonderful way to build a meaningful exchange.

Listen between the words. What can you learn from their body language? From their facial expressions? Their pauses? Just listen and give them the time they need to open up to you.

Watch your own body language. Face your child, pull up a chair, sit comfortably and lean in. Really focus on them as they talk to you and nod when appropriate. Be intentional with demonstrating your approachability, so make sure not to roll your eyes or cross your arms across your chest, which creates a feeling of tension. Try to relax your facial expression to appear calm and unthreatening.

Body language expert, Jessica Robinson, believes that a blend of verbal and non-verbal communication tools is required for us to connect in a proper manner. Speech, she says, becomes powerful when it is supported by suitable non-verbal aids like body language.

Be alert to moments of vulnerability and honesty. Whenever your teen starts talking openly and honestly, let them. Just listen. Don't judge them, and don't interrupt. They, too, need to vent their frustrations so give them the time they need to get everything off their chest.

Be genuinely interested in them. You may not be keen on the topic they're talking about, but you do care about them and that's what counts. Don't forget that your goal is to have them open up to you about their interests, their thoughts and emotions, whether that be about the argument in the schoolyard, the latest must-have fashion item or why one stream or computer game is better than the other. And the more you pay attention and ask clarifying questions, the more likely you are to become genuinely interested in their stories.

"Do you want me to give you suggestions or help? Or do you want me to just listen?"

Integrate this phrase as part of your repertoire for improving communication with your teen. They value our opinions and advice, but sometimes they just don't want to hear it — and we have to respect that.

> *This is a common phrase we use in our professional environments as part of the policies put in place by the educational establishments we work in. The phrase, "Do you want me to give you suggestions or help? Or do you want me to just listen?" allows the individual to offload any concerns without any*

*related stress. It reassures them that they won't
necessarily have to do anything about their
problem just yet, or that we won't be giving them
unsolicited advice on how to solve their issue.*

Choose the Right Language of Communication

Now that we know how to listen better, it's time to practice how to talk. We have to keep the communication channels open and flowing, and the old 'Do what I say' approach blocks off any chance of that. Teens want to be able to make their own decisions, with your loving guidance, and they certainly don't want every conversation to turn into a lesson or lecture.

In her article entitled *Deeper Conversations with Your Teen: The Questions You Need to Ask,* Gwen Edwards summarizes positive communication beautifully. Published on Focusonthefamily.ca

> "If you genuinely desire a close relationship with
> your teen, it may be time to learn a new
> parenting style – one perhaps best described as
> *the patient pursuit of your teen's heart.* It's a
> long-term process of creating the right
> 'relationship environment' for conversation,
> then waiting for your son or daughter to reveal
> what's *really* on their mind."

To do this, Edwards says your teen needs to feel that they are supremely important to you, that you are interested in their opinions and aspirations, and that you see — and love — the amazing adult they're becoming, even as they make mistakes along the way.

Here are some ways to facilitate that 'patient pursuit of your teen's heart.'

Talk with them, not at them. Teens no longer need us to talk to them as we did before, when we were teaching them the basics and concerned with their survival and safety. They don't want to feel controlled but want to feel valued, so talk about what interests them. Participate in their lives whenever you can — or whenever they let you. Grab any opportunity or invitation they throw your way and let yourself get silly and have fun. And why not try to be more flexible? Yes, you have rules, but if your son or daughter proves to you they can be responsible, they deserve to be given a chance and shown a little flexibility.

Watch your tone. It's not necessarily what we say that causes conflict, it's how we say it. It's crucial to pay attention to the pitch and tone of our voice when we communicate with our teens. They're very perceptive and can easily tell if we're annoyed — and sometimes we get annoyed at them for just being teens, which is unfair. (Remember, the logical part of their brains is not fully developed yet so they're not supposed to think as we do!) Changing the tone of our voices is something we, as teachers, are highly skilled at and we have found this to have a major impact on how students respond to us, their peers and their work. Also, choose your battles wisely. There will be conflict and disagreement, that's undeniable, but make an effort to keep things light — nobody wants to be arguing all the time. Choose what's worth arguing about. As for the rest, why not compliment them on their choices when it's deserved?

Encourage their efforts. Praise is an external motivator, whereas encouragement fosters internal motivation. Instead of telling them they're the best, try to encourage them to continue their personal growth. Let them know that you see the things they're doing right, not just what they're doing wrong. Try using phrases like the following to boost their spirits and motivate them further.

- "Thank you for your help. That really made a difference."
- "All that hard work paid off. You should be really proud of yourself."
- "I can tell you really care about..."
- "I trust your judgment on this."
- "I love working on this together with you."

Create a safe space for them to open up. Avoid distractions or other people listening in to your conversation. For planned, more serious discussions, provide something else for your teen to focus on if the situation becomes awkward. Being outside is a great idea because there's always a new view to take in, a bird to listen to, or a stone to pick up and throw. Go out and kick the ball together, or go for a walk. When there's physical movement, it's often easier for emotional movement and release to occur as well.

Spending time in the kitchen for meal prep or driving in the car together are also conducive for more improvised chats. Make a mental note when your teen says they like it somewhere — it means they feel comfortable there. Maybe go to that location for your future heart-to-heart chats.

Be observant. Try to pick up on your child's random comments. They may be too uncomfortable to talk about something serious and try to pass it off as unimportant — it's up to you to seize the moment. Also, be on the lookout for changes in their mood, behaviour, energy level or appetite. Similarly, if they stop wanting to do things that used to make them happy, start isolating themselves, or have a hard time functioning on a daily basis, ask them about it. This could be a sign of something more serious, so be supportive and don't judge them. They need to know they can trust you.

Don't judge, assume or accuse. It's okay to ask why, but always believe that your child had a good reason for their actions. Don't assume the worst, and don't overreact and turn things into catastrophes. Instead, remain calm, listen fully and try to understand their thinking process. Ask open questions like, "I'd love it if you could tell me what's been happening," and "I feel like something's bothering you."

Offer your help. Ask them if you can help, then leave it up to them to decide. If they do seek your assistance, make sure they know how you plan on helping them, and why. At this age, they like to feel in control of what concerns them. Teenagers need to start making decisions for themselves, so give them the time and space to think things through. Make sure they know you'll always be there for them.

According to Dr. Kenneth Ginsburg from the Center for Parent and Teen Communication, adolescents tend to divide things into several categories. They welcome adult input and interference when it comes to matters of safety, rules of society and universal morality.

As for the rest, the more personal stuff, they prefer we stay out — unless we've been asked our opinion, of course!

Watch your reactions. This is an important one. Do not do anything until both you and your teen are calm. If you need to take a time-out during a discussion, then do so. It's too easy to say things we'll regret when we're all fired up, and we can easily lose track or control of the direction we'd like the conversation to go. Explain to your child that things don't get resolved when angry, so it's best to take a breather, count to ten, maybe go out for a walk. You can go back to the discussion once everyone has had the chance to calm down.

Remember that you're the parent, so avoid any drama and don't react to anger with more anger or hurt. By remaining calm, it tells your teen that they're free to talk to you without fear of being judged. We all have moments when we're vulnerable and emotional too, but there's already enough drama going on in their adolescent lives — they certainly don't need any more coming from us. And don't take things too personally. When your teen tells you you're ruining their life, they don't really mean it. They're simply upset and are taking it out on you because you're there, which is likely something we, as parents, are sometimes guilty of too.

It's important to validate their feelings and agree with them when something is difficult, but don't over-empathize because that could also backfire. For example, if your teen comes home complaining that he had a run-in with his coach for forgetting his soccer boots, you can agree with him that he is feeling bad that he missed out on a sport that he loves. If you over-empathize, however, he may never learn to face the natural consequences of something like not packing his soccer boots. Try to stay as balanced as possible in situations like these.

Learn how to ask the right questions. Asking too many questions and being overprotective may feel like you're trying to control your teen, as if you don't trust them, and that can lead to lies.

Of course we want to know where they're going, who they're with and what they're doing, but for our teenagers, all these questions can seem too intrusive. This inquiring technique doesn't necessarily work, and as Dr. Kenneth

Ginsburg says, it's not what you ask, it's what you know — and what you know depends on what your child chooses to tell you.

So knowing how to be the kind of parent whose teen chooses to talk to them is one of the best ways to keep them safe and have a healthy relationship. The strategies outlined in this book will take you one step closer to becoming that kind of parent.

Teens tend to talk openly with parents who monitor safety and morality issues, but also give them freedom in other domains. This doesn't mean we don't want to know what's going on in other parts of their lives! The best way to get information from them is to ask open-ended instead of yes or no questions. "What would you do if you were in her shoes?" "Why do you think he reacted that way?" "How does that make you feel?"

Keeping things light is another effective way to get your teen to open up, or to simply be chattier. We've included some links to great conversation starters in the reference section at the back of the book, and here are some of our favourites.

- "What was the funniest thing that happened today?"
- "Which teacher at your school is the scariest? Why?"
- "Would you recommend any TV shows to me?"

- "What were the most memorable family trips we've taken so far? Where would you like to go next?"
- "Can you teach me how to text faster?"
- "Do you consider yourself an extrovert or introvert?"
- "What would you say motivates you?"
- "At what age do you think someone should be allowed to try alcohol?"
- "What are your opinions about marriage?"
- "Do you think teens have it easier or tougher compared to my generation?"

> *We have both tested many of these conversation starters on our own teens as well as our students, and we've found them to be highly effective in creating a positive, light-hearted dialogue full of engaging quality responses. These moments have allowed us to gain a better insight into our children's and students' personalities and passions as well as their general experiences and expectations.*

Improve Your General Relationship

Some teens need time to open up, while others need an actual invitation to talk. Make that effort to get to know their preferences and how your child responds best.

We've learned that the best way to communicate with anyone is by taking the time to do so. Time is the most precious thing we can give someone, whether that be listening to them or doing an activity together. And as much as it feels like our teens are pushing away, they actually do want some one-on-one time with us — only it has to be on their terms. Let them decide what you should do together. Try to unplug the electronic devices if you can.

Make your family values and expectations clear, sensible and fair. Discuss the consequences openly so your teen understands the 'why' behind them, and so that there are no surprises when rules get broken.

At the same time, respect your teen's boundaries. It can be hard to let go and give them the autonomy and privacy they're after, but they require their own space to grow, develop their judgment skills and make their own mistakes. With this in mind, it's a good idea to get to know their friends.

Kate often stays up late to have a chat with her son and his friends after they have been to a party.

Not only do we want to make sure that their friends are a good influence on them (or at least, not too much of a bad one!), but being part of your teen's social life can lead to a healthier relationship overall. And who knows, you may even find an activity that you all enjoy doing together.

Be a Good Example

As much as we encourage you to spend time together, don't make your adolescent feel like you require their validation to be a great parent. As soon as you need something from your child in order for you to feel better, you make yourself vulnerable because they don't have to please you every time. Fulfilling your needs is not your teenager's responsibility, so make every effort not to be a needy parent. Model the type of independent human you'd like your child to also become.

When you need something but don't get it, it's only natural to try harder by being more controlling and manipulating. In turn, your teen will become more and more defiant or passively compliant — neither of which is healthy. In reality, you don't need anyone else to prop you up. You can justify yourself and solve your own problems, so if your child is acting in a certain negative way, that's his problem. Your problem is to decide how you choose to react and behave toward him. That's in your control, not his.

Ask yourself, 'How do I want to act, no matter how my son or daughter is acting? What can I put up with and what can I not accept?' Take back your power and say to yourself, 'If my child is screaming at me, instead of needing them to stop, I can turn around and walk away, not engage.' Let your child know you won't talk with them until they can communicate with you in a civil manner. When you're not reacting and trying to control them, you will most likely see changes in their behaviour. This type of struggle that leads to personal development is a valuable experience for your teen to go through.

We got as far as their 13th birthdays believing we knew how our children thought and behaved.

But as they grew older, we've had to get to know them again and again — more deeply this time, and without judgment. We've raised them up to this point, and now it's time to witness how our words, values and actions, combined with their own opinions on life, have influenced who they are today. As teachers, authors and researchers, we continue to reflect on these factors because they are evolving and ever-changing.

Now remember, there's always room for improvement, and that rings true for everyone. Old habits can be hard to change, so be patient with yourself when you feel you have messed something up — because chances are, you will. We all do. It's important for our children to know this as well. We are all a work in progress, so admit your mistakes when they happen, and strive to improve in the future. The communication strategies outlined in this chapter are a good place to start.

You are the parent in this relationship, and while we are constantly learning invaluable lessons from our sons and daughters, our primary role remains to keep them safe and to prepare them to be kind, self-sufficient adults. As much as we'd like to become our teen's best friend, we still have to stand firmly in our role as their parents and mentors. In their eyes, we should represent a solid, stable and reliable sounding board whenever needed. Our calm, open-minded availability will take us one step further in the 'patient pursuit of our child's heart'.

Teenagers still need us to provide structure and discipline, support and guidance, but most of all, love. At this point in their lives, it's important to show a sincere appreciation for who they're becoming, for their growing knowledge, skills and socio-emotional development. For the most whole-hearted connection, however, it's not enough to just show them these things — we should embody them completely and aspire to feel truly appreciative of this human we are preparing to let fly into the great world.

FIVE

DEALING WITH DAY-TO-DAY TEEN ISSUES

L azy? Rude? Too dependent? Do any (or all) of these adjectives describe your son or daughter right now? You are not alone. These, and more, are normal issues that most of us have with our teens, and the fact that your teen is disrespectful or messy certainly doesn't mean you're a bad parent.

Put yourself in their shoes. Recall that their brains don't work the same way ours do, and instead of reason and logic, they're ruled by their impulses and emotions. That's why they're often very intense, moody and impatient.

By testing our limits and talking back, for example, they're seeing just how far they can go in being different from us — they're testing their independence. And when they're moody, it's normal. We often like to blame that on hormones, but it's really much more than that.

At their age, not only are they trying to figure out how the world works, but they're striving to find out where they fit in it. Appearances are super important and our teens are trying so hard to look and be 'cool'. Dealing with the pressures of school, friends, social media, that's hard work! It's no wonder they're tired and moody when they get home. And what do they do then? They take it out on us because, deep down, they know we'll always love them and be there for them. (We should never stop reminding them of that!)

There's no one-size-fits-all method when dealing with these types of adolescent issues, but there are several proven ways to reduce the stress and frustrations that come with our perfectly imperfect teens.

It's up to us as parents to be creative and use a variety of the strategies outlined below to smooth out whatever situation we're having. As long as calm and patience, love and respect are in the mix as you begin to implement the strategies outlined in this book, you'll soon begin to notice a welcomed change in your relationship.

How to Motivate Your Lazy Teen

How long does it take for your teen to do something? Homework? Chores?

Lack of motivation for things that are not fun is perfectly normal in teens. Ask yourself honestly, how motivated are you to do something you don't enjoy? Thanks to our developed prefrontal cortex, however, we know that certain things need to get done, and so we accept and do them more willingly than our children do. But teens don't have this knowledge or experience yet, so they put off what they don't feel like doing.

If you think that your child is lazy, the first thing to rule out is any health issues. Make sure that their laziness is not a sign of something bigger, like overwhelming stress, depression or anxiety — conditions that are sadly more and more prevalent these days.

For them to stay healthy, we have to ensure that our sons and daughters get enough sleep. At their age, teens are still developing and need eight to ten hours of sleep every night. Most of them are not getting that much. Staying out late too many nights a week with friends or at parties, alcohol consumption, and gaming or messaging friends until 4 am are just some of the reasons modern-day adolescents do not get enough sleep. It's only normal then that they act miserably and feel unmotivated because that's what sleep deprivation does. As much as possible, try to get them to stick to a routine, just as you did when your child was an infant or junior. The routine will shift to become a slightly later bedtime routine, but the main idea is to keep timings regular — especially during the school week.

Screen time also affects how active they are. Digital distraction has become a serious problem, and our children's young brains are easily tempted and, *yes*, addicted to technology. Why would they want to clean their room when they can just push a button, sit back and be entertained?

Set clear boundaries. Together, come to a compromise on the amount of time they are allowed to spend on their devices. And no, it's not too harsh to take away their phones at night. You will likely get a tantrum once you do this, (as well as a few days of sulking), but make it clear to them that their growing bodies need to get sufficient sleep. Explain to them that the light from their devices is a stimulant that affects their ability to fall and stay asleep, and that their brains need to relax for at least an hour before going to bed. They will thank you for this in the long run.

Encourage your teens to go outside and do something physical. Being active and fresh air are two great ways to keep them both physically and mentally healthy — not to mention that it will help them sleep much better. This does not have to be exercise per se. It can be a quick visit to the shops, a spot of lawn mowing, pruning the hedges, cleaning the car, painting a fence or anything else that gets them outdoors and moving.

We can sometimes feel like we have to coerce our teens into action, but as you've probably learned by now, forcing anyone to do anything leads to long faces and negative vibes — and often bad results.

Easier and more effective than forcing is motivating. Now, we certainly don't want to be bribing our teens, but almost...

> *Liz has discovered that it can take a whole weekend for her teen daughters to tidy out their old clothes and rooms in general. At one point, it seemed that there would be nothing Liz could implement to hurry this process along, until she tried a new strategy — motivation! Giving them a clear incentive to go out on a shopping spree to update their wardrobes was the saving grace method that worked for them. This way, she learned that she could hurry up the process and change the way they thought about the chore.*

By the time your son or daughter is an older teen, they should have developed good habits with regards to all of the points above. But if you are using this book to help your older teen, it is worth discussing with them all of the ideas outlined here then giving them the independence to put them into place in a way that works for them.

The Premack Principle

In the mid-20th century, psychologist David Premack discovered that *preferred* behaviours can be used to reinforce *unpreferred* behaviours. In order words, before we can do something we enjoy, like playing a video game, for example, we have to complete something we don't enjoy, like finishing our daily chores or homework.

As adults, this is something most of us do naturally; we wash the dishes before we sit down for a movie. For teens, on the other hand, this act of self-discipline is something that needs to be practiced, over and over and over again. Applying the Premack Principle is an excellent way for them to learn some of the personal responsibility and accountability they'll need to make it out on their own.

In order for this principle to work, however, we need to follow certain guidelines.

Establish clear house rules. Sit down as a family and discuss who is responsible for what. Let your teen select the chores they'd rather do and decide on a realistic schedule for which they'll get everything done, including schoolwork and other planned activities. Write everything down and put it in a visible place. You can even create a contract, which everyone signs and agrees upon. Make sure the consequences for not getting things done are clear and part of your agreement.

Be consistent. This is one of the most important guidelines in parenting children of any age: when we say we're going to do something, we do it. We have to follow through with the rules and consequences even when we're tired and frustrated of repeating the same things over and over again. And soon enough, our diligent persistence will pay off. Our reminders will become less and less frequent as our teens develop the good habit of responsibility.

Remember that this process will be much easier if our teens understand the reasons behind having to do something. 'Because I said so' is no longer valid. The 'why' behind a task has to be important to them as well, and not just to us as parents. Teens will be more driven if they can understand and see the beneficial results in the long run.

Seven Tips for Dealing with a Disrespectful Teenager

Teen expert Daniel Wong states that lack of respect is often a way of getting attention, of telling us that they don't feel accepted. Our teen's indifference can also be a cover-up for their struggles, or simply a way for them to avoid doing what they're supposed to be doing.

As teens leave behind their childhoods, they tend to feel insecure and powerless, which is only normal considering all the uncertainties and mysteries of impending adulthood.

In order to give themselves more power, adolescents feel the need to separate and differentiate themselves from their parents. Standing apart from their family and acting in a way that's opposite to what they've been shown naturally causes confrontation, which often leads to the infamous parent-teen power struggle. And power struggles are never a good use of time and energy.

As our sons and daughters focus on learning to stand up for their ideals and express themselves as adults, they may not always be paying attention to their tone or choice of words.

Here are some of Daniel Wong's suggestions for dealing with disrespectful teens which Kate and Liz have implemented themselves. The approaches below are strategies that have worked exceptionally well in improving their day-to-day interactions with their adolescents.

1. **Establish the rules and boundaries.** Make the decisions as a family —although remember that you, the parent, have the final word. **No swearing, no name-calling, no threats**. Write it all down, along with the consequences for breach of respect, then make sure to reinforce these when need be.

2. **Stay calm.** By now, they know how to push your buttons, just like you know how to push theirs. **Don't let yourself get involved in an unnecessary argument** with an explosive, verbally abusive teen, and tell them you'll talk about this once they've cooled down. Calmly tell them that you don't like it when they speak to you like that, and that the rules won't change just because they yell and argue about them. **Have them take a break,** count to ten, and get their ideas (and tone of voice) straight before continuing the discussion.

3. **Ignore the small stuff.** Sometimes it's best to **dismiss a discontented shrug, slammed door or inappropriate comment**. In fact, they may even be doing these on purpose, just to irritate you. We want our children to be able to express all their emotions openly, and an eye roll is a fairly innocent way for them to show their

disagreement or discontent. As long as they're not stepping over the line of what's appropriate in your household, **simply take a deep breath and let it pass.**

4. **Be a role model.** Our teens may seem to be ignoring us, but they're silently observing everything we do. If you explode anytime something goes wrong, how can you expect anything different from them? **Set the example of how to behave properly** by showing loving patience and respect for everyone, even in difficult situations. And don't let yourself get worked up by the little things. Try to **remain calm and balanced.** Speak clearly and without accusation, and **use positive language** when possible. Instead of saying things like "You really messed up this time," or "You should learn how to treat people better," try turning the statement around to reflect how *you* feel about their behaviour. "It makes me feel attacked when you talk to me like that," or "I get the impression that something bigger is going on with you. I'd love it if you could confide in me." And although they may be acting like a jerk, they are generally willing to learn from you and your example.

5. **Give a warning followed by clear expectations.** We all inadvertently step out of bounds, so it's only fair for us to give our kids a chance. But if they've had a clear warning and know exactly what is expected from them and then still go on to display disrespectful behaviour, it's time to enact the consequences. "If you

continue winding your sister up now, time will come out of your free time to reflect and write an apology." "For the sake of everyone's safety, you know I expect calm, civilized behaviour in the car so that the driver can focus on the road rather than on the argument in the back seat. If you don't calm down now, you will miss the next gathering with your mates."

6. **Be consistent with the consequences.** Being consistent is often one of the most difficult aspects of parenting. We zealously establish the rules of the home, then become slack or don't always follow through with our decisions. As parents, we get fed up with repeating the same things over and over again, but if we can be constant and stick through it for a while, we'll see that it pays off — and often more quickly than we may expect. Also, **make the consequences short-term.** There's no need for punishment to drag on and on. By keeping things short, teens have a chance to learn quickly, go back out into the world and try again. Finally, there's no need to turn the knife in the wound by saying things like "I knew this would happen," or "I told you so." This will only make them angrier and resentful, so **let the consequences speak for themselves.**

7. **Don't be too harsh.** Remind your teen that you're enforcing these consequences for their own good, out of love, and in hopes that they'll learn from their mistakes. But even with all these positive intentions, it's hard to judge if our consequences are fair, or if they'll even pay off in the end. To try to keep some semblance of control,

many parents tend to be overly strict, which often leads to teens lying, no longer bringing friends home and avoiding communication altogether — and as parents, this is the last thing we want.

So how can we tell if we're being too harsh? Ask yourself these questions: Do I have more rules than other parents, and are some of them there only 'because I said so'? Do I nag and act dissatisfied all the time? Are my threats over-the-top and unrealistic? Am I flexible enough with the things neither my teen nor I can control? Are my expectations of how I'd like my teen to behave reasonable? Am I trying to control them, or am I guiding them and giving them the tools they need to become the best version of themselves? Do I really listen when my child talks? Do I let them express themselves freely, even if I disagree with their point of view? Am I going to regret the way I have spoken to or reacted to my child? Reflect on these questions, then make the adjustments you need to become a fairer, more coherent parent.

Dealing with Teens Who Keep Pushing the Boundaries and Breaking the Rules

Teenagers need to understand where the boundaries are, which is why they're often testing and pushing them. Yet when they push too far, they need to learn to deal with the consequences. But what if we helped them reduce the instances in which they push us too far?

When looking at the principles of positive parenting, guidance stands out as the best form of discipline. We shouldn't try to control our teens. Instead, we should practice guiding our children to do the right thing, understanding why they act the way they do, and teaching them instead of punishing them. In fact, punishment can make them feel afraid, humiliated and hurt — emotions that are not conducive to strengthening your bond or their personal development.

On the other hand, when we guide our teens, it means we're willing to work with them to find solutions. It shows them that we trust them and know they can do better — and that we're willing to cooperate to help them get there. Positive parenting is something we should all strive for, and it's better to start practicing it now than never. And when we're talking about parenting teens, this positive approach puts us on a more even playing ground, getting us ready for the adult relationship we will soon have with our child.

When children misbehave, we tend to believe that they're looking for attention, and often they are. But more than attention, it's the connection they're after.

According to Alfred Adler, the psychiatrist and philosopher who developed the concept of positive discipline, we're all constantly seeking to belong to a group and feel significant in our relationships. Without maybe realizing it, our teens are striving to contribute to their relationships and feel the joy that comes from human connection.

So when they misbehave and push the boundaries, maybe they're trying to connect with their peers. If, as parents, we make a greater effort to connect with them on a positive level, on their level, we can fulfill part of their needs for connection. By being cooperative with them, it also lets them know that they can trust and turn to us when needed. Teach them, then trust that they're learning from their mistakes or bad behaviour. This supportive cycle should lead to fewer reasons for them to misbehave in the first place.

Let's take an extreme but realistic example of alcohol and drugs. At some point during their adolescence, they are likely to be exposed to or offered these substances, or feel pressured to conform in a friendship group. No parent wants to imagine their children pushing the boundaries to the point of consuming alcohol when underage, or taking drugs to the point of addiction. Still, at this time in their lives they might try one of these substances we don't necessarily approve of. Experimenting is a normal part of growing up, but what should we do to prevent these experiments from becoming a problem?

The first thing is to talk openly about the subject at home. Explain to your teens what each substance can do, and what the dangers are of becoming addicted to them. They are more likely to turn to you for help and advice if they feel they won't be judged or reprimanded.

Next, keep an eye out for physical and psychological signs that your teen might be using drugs or alcohol. Changes in eating and sleeping habits, feeling physically ill and shaky, weight loss or gain, mood swings, loss of interest in favourite activities, changes in friendships, anxiety, anger, withdrawal... These are some of the signs that it is time to intervene and start asking questions.

> *A parent we worked with told us about his son's experience with drugs. Having entered his sophomore year, he began to drift from his usual friendship group with whom he'd had a close connection since first grade. Along with this, his school grades began to drop and he was going out of his way to do paid jobs without necessarily committing to one particular job. It was only when one of his old friends saw him at a party taking cocaine that the parents were informed and could step in to help him. Luckily for everyone, they had caught the addiction problem in its beginnings and the rehabilitation process was fairly straightforward.*

Recognizing the problem is the first step towards finding a solution. Be supportive and understanding, and if needed, get some professional help and advice. Overcoming addiction is not easy, and the sooner you acknowledge something is wrong, the better it will be for your teen. And if your efforts at home are not enough, seek outside recovery from your doctor or health advisor.

Open discussion, support and understanding are also effective in dealing with other examples of teens pushing the boundaries.

What About When They Don't Listen?

Teens often ignore us and pretend they don't hear us talking to them. They know this makes us feel powerless because making sure they're actively listening is something we can't physically do. It's out of our control, and they know that. So what should we do when our teens don't listen?

First, **find the right moment to talk about important things.** When someone is worked-up or upset, or simply busy and in the middle of something else, it's unlikely they'll listen or try to understand different points of view.

> *One of our school parents found that there was little point in discussing how late his older teen had come home after a party because he was tipsy from drinking and not thinking straight. Instead, he ensured his son had safely gone to bed and waited for a good time the next morning to communicate his concerns about this behaviour.*

React calmly. In the midst of a drama, wait until they've cooled down and are receptive to come back to the issue. Be respectful of their feelings and the fact that they are upset, and take the time to listen to them. (We can't stress this enough!) Don't judge your teen for their behaviour. Once you've shown a balanced, respectful response towards them, they are more likely to do the same to you.

Stay focused on your goal. What is it you want your child to learn from this situation? Don't let yourself be distracted by their growing repertoire of distraction tactics. Remain clear and direct with your words, and stick to the facts, not the emotions associated with the situation. If they try to pull you into a power struggle, remind them that you're not getting involved with that, and leave the room. Come back to the topic later.

Feel free to **remind them that they know the rules** because, hey, there they are, posted on the fridge. This could be related to how they speak to you, the way they are dressing for parties, not keeping to curfew timings, not being clear about where they are or simply not completing their agreed household duties. Until they've proven that they can follow the rules you established together, there's no reason to change or debate them.

And yes, if they don't have headphones on and are within hearing distance, you can assume that they hear everything you're saying. The more you ask them, "Are you listening to me? Did you hear what I just said?", the more they'll want to roll their eyes or slam the door. Keep your message clear and only tell them important things when you're sure they will hear you.

It's time to stop rescuing your child and show them ways to become more independent. Try not to make decisions for your teens, but instead teach them how to make the best decisions for themselves. Encourage negotiation and open discussions on mature topics like ethics, religion, politics and planning for the future, and talk to them without preaching. Their opinions are valid, so don't judge.

At this stage of parenthood, our role is to teach them valuable life skills that will launch them safely and successfully into adulthood, so it's important to be purposeful and deliberate in the ways we provide guidance. **"Am I helping my teen learn something and improve?"** This question should always be kept top of mind.

There are three main types of independence we should strive to prepare our teens for: emotional, behavioural and value-based independence.

Emotional independence comes from being able to face problems, react to them and find solutions on our own. It means being able to regulate our feelings and know if we're over-reacting.

Behavioural autonomy means being able to make decisions and follow through with the most appropriate actions. As we learn to think more abstractly, we're better able to weigh the pros and cons of each situation. We act a certain way because we believe it's right, not just because others are doing it too.

Value-based independence refers to being able to formulate our own ideas regarding spiritual, political and moral beliefs. We question what we're told and are able to defend our opinions without hurting others.

And how do we promote these three types of independence? Through practice and encouragement.

Empowering Teens Towards Independence

Learning to manage their own schedule, complete their chores and make well-founded decisions surrounding unexpected events are life skills that will empower your teens. Children become overly dependent when they don't feel confident enough to do certain things, which is often a result of parents not expecting much of them in that specific department. Traditional schools don't necessarily teach valuable life skills, so how will your teen learn how to do laundry, or save money, if they've never had to?

Can your teen cook for themselves? Can they take care of important errands around town? Can they drive yet? Can they make their own journey to and from places on public transportation? Do they get nervous when left alone in social situations?

Explain to them the freedom that comes with being able to do these kinds of things on their own, then look at the areas in which you and your teen feel there is too much dependence. Now, discern which knowledge and skills they need in order for them to be able to do these things, then set about teaching them hands-on. Once they seem comfortable enough to do something on their own, push them out of their comfort zone and let them go practice in the real world.

By learning new skills, little by little, your teen will overcome their fears, become more confident and may soon begin to enjoy the freedom that comes with being self-reliant. And as a parent, you'll feel calmer knowing they're better equipped to make it on their own.

Five Steps to Help Build Their Skills

Teens fear failure and often feel vulnerable regarding their future. They may go from being self-assured in one aspect of their lives to highly insecure in another. The best thing we can do for them is to teach them valuable life skills that will take them confidently into adulthood. Here's how.

1. **Get them thinking.** Make them a part of your adult conversations and ask for their opinions on important matters. Together, try to identify their feelings and the reasons behind them. After listening to them, feel free to share your own feelings and impressions. At this point in their lives, teens are trying to understand how their behaviours affect those around them, and the

implications behind their actions. **Ask them what they think their friends would do in this situation.** Being able to reflect on their emotions, put these into words and talk openly about them are all invaluable steps towards clear communication.

2. **Teach through interaction.** The goal for them is to learn new skills and behaviours while replacing old ones. Teach them concrete ways to cope with complicated situations, be that by demonstrating problem-solving techniques (like how to prepare a dessert for guests, what to do when the dog goes missing, or how to react if they witness an accident) and providing methods for them to calm themselves down. Think about why you do things a certain way, and if that's the best way for them to do things as well. Is there a better solution? Discuss your thought process openly with them — this will give them insight into how different people react to circumstances, as well as teach them adaptability. It will also allow them to see that you're just a normal person too, which may make them feel more comfortable opening up to you.

3. **Practice new life skills.** Show them how to do things then coach them when they attempt to do it by themselves. Recognize their efforts and make sure to tell them that you noticed their progress, no matter how small. This will give them the confidence to keep trying. Get them involved in their community and engage them in a joint cause, like a food collection, raising funds for the local shelter, or a charity walk, run or cycle.

4. **Support their development.** Teens will rarely get things right the first time around, so be there to teach and explain things as often as need be. Your patience and your belief in them are key to having them try again. Fix what's been broken together, and focus on maintaining a supportive and loving relationship.

5. **Recognize their progress.** Remark on their efforts and remember that these are more important than the results. Even the smallest improvements deserve to be recognized, so be specific in your praise. "I noticed that you cleaned up your room without me having to ask, and I really appreciate that. You should be proud of yourself for taking care of your stuff!" "I'm really glad you came home on time last night as this shows we can trust you." "That's brilliant that you completed all your homework before we all went to dinner because now you don't have to think about it." Make it a habit to celebrate their successes, even if it's just with an ice cream and a big hug.

How to Negotiate With Your Teen

According to The Successful Parent website, negotiation is a valuable tool that teaches teens skills they can use in all types of situations. These skills include the capacity to express their thoughts and feelings, the ability to think more objectively, self-awareness and consideration of others, cooperative problem-solving approaches and brainstorming creative solutions. Talking things out on a mature level also helps build trust and avoid unnecessary power struggles. What's more, teens who feel comfortable disagreeing and persuading others calmly are more likely to be able to resist negative peer pressure later on. Negotiation is indeed a powerful skill!

The best way to negotiate is to consider what each person wants or needs, then figure out how to make that happen. The correct way to do this is by compromising and reaching a middle ground, trying to attain a win-win situation for both parties.

Be careful though, as there are two ways to negotiate. Instead of negotiating *with* you, some teens tend to negotiate *around* you. Our kids don't necessarily want to compromise, so instead they've figured out how to work around you when you're standing in the way of their plans. This is especially common with defiant, head-strong teens who have the unpleasant ability to wear you down until you break. Now, we've all been there, too tired to stick to our guns, and sometimes it just seems easier to give in.

Once you have said 'no', however, don't change your answer to 'yes', unless you've received new information and you really do believe that your answer should now be 'yes'. Kids will hassle their parents to exhaustion, until we change our mind — but that teaches them that their strategies, whether that's arguing, crying or non-stop hounding, work, and those are negative patterns to fall into. It's best to stand firm in our decision. You can even explain and admit to them that you responded too quickly this time, that maybe you didn't give the right response, but that next time you promise to be more thoughtful.

Reflect on why you're leaning towards saying 'no' this time. Is there a valid reason why your teen's request should not receive a 'yes'? Parents tend to blurt out 'no' before even really thinking about the reasons why, so try to be more conscious of how you interact with your teen. Make sure to take the time to consider all the angles of a situation and formulate your thoughts before responding. Listen to everything your child has to say, and if you don't know how to answer just yet, tell them that you'll respond shortly.

Here are some other strategies we have used to help in our negotiations with teens.

Set the Tone

As we've learned by now, it's important for both parties to remain calm and respectful. It's our role as parents to set the tone, and to prompt our teens with **"Please tell me what you want or need, and why."**

Take turns to **listen to what the other is saying**, without interruption, and **rephrase to make sure you understand properly**. Of course it's important to show and talk about emotions, but do so without attitude, sarcasm or resentment. If you or your teen are getting worked up, it's better to continue the discussion once everyone has cooled down.

If possible, **get ready for the discussion in advance.** For teens, thinking about their end goals and preparing their arguments for how to reach these goals beforehand will help them think abstractly and build more coherent thoughts. They'll also be less nervous when confronting you.

As parents, get all the details from them and ask as many questions as possible. Not only will this make the situation clearer in your mind, but it will also help them fill in the blanks and see the situation from more angles than they may be used to. This is a valuable way for them to learn all the elements involved in adult decision-making.

Reach a Compromise Everyone is Happy With

As always, it helps if both parents are on the same side and show a united front. If they don't agree, they may have to negotiate together before starting to negotiate with their teen.

Either way, **let your teen see that you're trying to help them get what they want**, as long as it's reasonable. But it's also important that your concerns and feelings are met and respected. Remember, you've got more experience than they do, so what would you, the parent, need, before being able to come to some sort of agreement?

Get as much information out on the table as possible, and together, brainstorm all the options and possible solutions. Try to meet somewhere in the middle, and give a little if you can. Take your child's past behaviours into consideration; you may be more flexible if they've shown they can be trusted. Likewise, you may have to set stricter guidelines until they can prove that they've learned from their previous mistakes. Remind them that they can earn more freedom and flexibility by demonstrating that they are able to make good choices.

Repeat the Compromise then State the Consequences

"I don't mind if you start wearing make-up to school, but I'd like you to use safe, good quality products on your face. You also have to wash your face properly before going to bed. If I see that you're not doing that, I'll take away your make-up. And don't forget that there is always the likelihood that you will be instructed by school staff not to wear make-up again."

"You can go to Paul's party tonight, but only if you promise to finish your homework before tomorrow afternoon. If you don't finish your work by then, you won't be able to go to tomorrow's game."

"I am not keen on you wearing those ripped jeans and midriff top to grandma's birthday dinner, but I don't mind if you wear that outfit when you go out with your friends for a meal."

Your teens may not be completely happy with the outcome, and disappointment is normal since things didn't go as they'd envisioned. Give them time to accept your decision. Once you've stated the benefits of this compromise, there's no need to repeat them unless they ask you to.

Sometimes we have to make unpopular decisions and certain things are just not negotiable, like skipping school or drunk driving. Be firm in your decisions. "I'll let you go to the dance on Saturday, but no drinking, and I'm coming to pick you up at midnight."

How we respond to negotiation depends greatly on how old our child is — our permissions for our 13-year-old will be much different than for our 16-year-old.

> *One of our parents found this process of reaching a compromise through detailed discussion incredibly effective when she discovered that her teen had been sneaking his girlfriend into the house after everyone had gone to bed. She reported initial arguments and rising tensions along with worries about sex and safety. Once she put our suggested negotiation approach into practice, she found the results were far better as they reached the compromise of her son's girlfriend visiting the house once a week at set times.*

Teens often feel like they're at war with their parents, so it's important for them to know that you're all on the same team and that you all want what's best for the family. Teen expert Daniel Wong suggests not taking our child's actions too personally; it's too easy to get overly emotional when we take things to heart.

He says that we should focus on their behaviour, and not on the person. Our teens are not lazy or disrespectful, they just behave this way; their behaviours are much easier to change than their innate characteristics. Approach these issues with understanding and patience (no matter how hard that may seem!), and let your teens know they are loved.

They don't want to be seen with you anymore? They duck in the car or walk behind you on the street? Our sons and daughters are often more embarrassed of us than we are of them, but again, don't take this personally. It's their way of practicing separation and individuality. Still, keep inviting them to join you in activities, even if they keep saying no. They may surprise you one day...

But for now, your reaction is often the only thing you can control at this point. Start by focusing on one conscious parenting tip at a time. When you have that one aspect under control, implement another.

SIX

THE MOST EFFECTIVE WAYS TO DEAL WITH CONFLICT

C onflicts arise out of problems, or when teen issues get out of hand. They also occur to teach us a lesson and inspire us to improve for the future. They're a natural part of growth so rest assured: conflict in the home is absolutely normal.

While we do not enjoy the tension and should try to limit these often negative situations, there are some unexpected benefits to disagreeing and arguing with your teen. We've already looked at the benefits of clear communication, negotiation and compromise, but conflict also teaches anger management, dealing with disappointment and resilience. These are all valuable life skills that are best practiced in a loving family environment.

In previous chapters, we learned that adolescents don't respond well to too much parental control, yet they still need us to behave like parents in certain parts of the game. This means we need to maintain some level of authority over them, but how much is too much? Or what's considered not enough? Finding the right balance as parents can be difficult, and when combined with the fact that our increasingly independent kids don't yet see the world with the same reasoning as we do, it's no wonder clashes occur.

Indeed, building discipline in the pre-teen years will give you a head start. If you set a benchmark of your expectations and standards of behavior from your child, and at the same time model this daily, these become non-negotiable. You all expect a certain level of respect and behaviour from one another. Furthermore, it is not too late to introduce non-negotiables even if your children are older teens.

In this chapter, we'll cover some useful and simple strategies to deal with conflicting situations. But first, let's examine a few of the reasons why we struggle to hold on to control.

Why Parents Want Control

Throughout our child's life, we've done what we could to help them grow into adulthood as their best selves. And although some of us think it is, it's not solely our responsibility to make sure our children turn out 'right'.

They are their own human beings, separate from us, and the sooner we understand this, the better. Soon we'll have to completely let go, to disconnect from our authoritative role, and begin to follow the flow of where our now-young adult is headed.

But until then, what keeps us so worried and longing for control?

The teen brain is still in development. We now know that our child's brain is not fully ready to make wise, logical decisions until they're well into their 20s. Their neuropsychological capabilities are not fully developed, although they probably don't know that yet. Our teens are still part child, but act oh-so-ready to become adults.

Of course this makes it hard for us to feel 100% confident when our 18-year-old starts driving, or moves out of the house. We know they're not fully ready yet, but as with parenting, adulthood is something you're never quite prepared for. You learn these things on the fly. Our biggest hope is that we've given them a solid foundation for building a safe and happy life.

Modern culture does not support our values. And this is truer now than ever. So-called society is constantly pulling us in different directions, and as much as growing up sounds exciting, it also comes with heavy responsibilities that our little ones are scared to take on. They feel torn between the comforts of home and the responsibilities that come with leaving home, and we can't blame them — they've seen all the issues we as adults have to deal with.

From an early age, our sons and daughters are bombarded with depictions of drinking and sex, for instance, and other expectations of how young people should act, and often, these contradict what they learned in the home. With what the media says and the ensuing peer pressure, these behavioural choices are hard to face. It's no wonder our teens are reluctant, confused, or downright terrified to have to make these decisions. And as parents, we're just as nervous and afraid as they are. What's more, we're not used to the modern way in which teens socialize today. Most of us grew up with face-to-face meet-ups and real conversations as opposed to virtual connections on Snapchat and TikTok.

Teens are over-stimulated and sleep-deprived. Unless we're consciously taking the time to unplug from the fast-paced world and enjoy the quiet, we've all got too much on our minds. So many of us are stressed, and the easy access and growing addiction to technology and social media certainly don't help. When we don't sleep well or take care of ourselves, we become anxious and impatient, which leads to poor decision-making and mistakes. As adults, we may have developed self-care strategies and tools to deal with an uncertain, agitated world, but many of our teens have not.

Parents want to live out their dreams through their teens. It's unfair to expect our children to have the same goals and desires as we do, or to do what we wish we had done when we were their age. Hopefully we've raised our sons and daughters to be their own independent beings, with their own strengths and weaknesses, likes and dislikes.

We need to respect them for who they are. Along the same line, we shouldn't worry too much about them making the same mistakes we did. So much has changed since we were their age, and they'll need to surpass their own hardships and learn for themselves.

Understanding Why Parent and Teen Conflict Occurs

Conflict is not always as simple as an argument. It's actually what happens right before the argument, when two people disagree on something. And when it comes to parents and teens, we all know there's a lot to disagree on, from our perception of lazy to disrespectful attitudes, and more.

We may feel disappointed, ashamed or embarrassed by our teen's behaviour. And let's face it, they're going to embarrass you in life — but likely not as much as you embarrass them. Learning to deal with shame and disappointment is an ongoing process that can only be overcome through the motions of the experience.

Hot Topics

> *In our households, the hot topics of discussion often revolve around the use of electronics, chores, not spending enough time with the family, school, homework, too many late nights, not sticking to curfews, physical appearance, choice of friends, going out too much, disrespect towards family members, dishonesty... The list goes on.*

In fact, the causes for conflict between parents and teens have existed for as long as humanity has — only the superficial specifics differ. In 1983, Dr. Raymond Montemayor published an aptly-named study in the *Journal of Early Adolescence*, Parents and Adolescents in Conflict: All Families Some of the Time and Some Families Most of the Time. The context of raising children has certainly changed since the early 80s, but when it comes to family battles and power struggles, the fundamental causes are the same.

"According to some, the young and old are engaged in a continual and oftentimes heated generational conflict that pits energy and idealism against wisdom and realism."

Dr. Montemayor goes on to explain that the conflict often lies here: **"... life must be experienced and the knowledge of the old may serve as only a partial guide for the young, to the continual dismay of parents."**

We wish our teens would listen to us, but that doesn't mean they will. So how should we proceed when their energetic and emotional idealism conflicts with the wisdom we've gained from our own past experiences?

Seven Essential Strategies to Manage Parent-Teen Conflict

It's crucial to manage parent-teen conflicts carefully, because if the process of working through them is not constructive, there could be negative consequences for the family going forward.

As parents, we need to model the best ways to handle situations, especially the most difficult ones. How we deal with our own mistakes will reflect on how our teens deal with theirs in the future. Here are some of the best ways to deal with conflict which we have found to be very effective.

Count to ten to calm down. First and foremost, we all need to cool down, and a surefire way to do this is through deep breathing and counting to ten. You may have used this technique when your child was younger, maybe as early as when they were two or three years old and throwing their first tantrums. Teenagers often resemble toddlers when they're angry, so now it's time to bring this very simple, yet often overlooked strategy to the forefront and recall the benefits that conscious breathing has on conflict resolution.

Counting to ten should be the first thing parents do before approaching any disagreement. It gives us time to cool down and get our thoughts in order. Deep breathing reduces aggression and prevents us from lashing out too harshly at our teen, and vice versa — which is often what happens in the heat of the moment.

As parents, it's difficult not to overreact, but still, we may have more self-control than our teens do in these impassioned situations. It's our role to help them see and understand the value of this intentional pause. By teaching our teens how to self-regulate their emotions in times of conflict and crisis, we're giving them one of the most valuable tools to deal with what can be an overwhelming world.

Finally, it's okay to disengage completely from an argument if your teen won't stop ranting. Simply tell them that you've had enough of the futile discussion and that you'll be happy to find a solution once they've cooled down.

Think before you speak. After you've taken several deep breaths and calmed down, try to express yourself with clear, honest and specific requests. Be intentional in your choice of words and talk constructively. There should be no name-calling, no swearing, no criticizing. Do your best to keep your tone of voice down and ask open-ended questions.

Use 'I statements' whenever possible. "I feel disappointed when I see that you don't do the things you said you would." "I become worried when you don't come home at the time we agreed on." "I get the impression that you don't care about my feelings when you shout at me like that."

It's also imperative for everyone to be given the space to express exactly how they feel, both in the negative and positive sense. By acknowledging the upside of a conflict, it stops the dynamic from becoming defined solely by negativity. Of course, it can be difficult to see the bright side of things during a discussion that started off as fury, but it could be as simple as recognizing the valuable lessons learned from the event. "I'm happy that we had this argument because now I know that it hurts you when I act like this." "I'm glad we talked about our feelings before things got even more out of hand."

Keep the past in the past. We've all made our share of mistakes, which we've hopefully learned from and improved on. Teenagers evolve at an astronomical rate, so in most cases, it's unreasonable to relate what is happening now to what happened six months ago, or even last week. They adapt quickly to situations and develop depending on how we relate to them.

That's why it's important not to project our own inner critic onto our children. As we saw from our self-reflection exercises in Chapter 3, a lot of our innate behaviours come from our past, more specifically from the way we were dealt with when we were young. Without meaning to, we pass our own beliefs, habits and life experiences onto our kids, which may or may not be beneficial to them. By being aware of this and consciously working on improving ourselves and breaking our negative patterns, not only do we set a positive example for our teens, but we leave the past in the past and focus on the present.

Address the real issue and focus on common objectives. Why exactly are you arguing? Emotions often exaggerate your differences, so strive to push your feelings aside and pinpoint the real reason for this clash. Can you address the actual issue? Is your teen being disrespectful because they're disappointed in your decision? Have they done something to break your trust, or were your expectations too high? Or are they just being moody because they're tired after a long week at school? Once the issue is clear in your mind, ask yourself if the fight is even worth it. As a parent of teens, we need to choose our battles wisely and allow them to learn from their own mistakes. So is what they're doing dangerous? Does it go against your family values? Will the outcome really cost you your relationship or have long-term consequences for your family? Always look at the bigger picture and try to be objective.

Remember that you're a family, not the enemy. You both want what's best for the other, so focus on the goals you set together and the reasons for doing so. Most of these goals likely include staying safe and helping your teen become the best version of themselves. This will help you put the situation into perspective.

Brainstorm and decide on solutions together. Get creative and think about ways you can resolve the issues together. Ask your teen what they would like to see happen. Stay open-minded to their ideas, no matter how silly or unreasonable they may seem, and don't judge them. Chances are you'll both have to compromise and fine-tune your negotiation skills before coming to a solution, and that's good practice — especially for them.

Remember, it's still considered a conflict if one or the other feels unheard or dismissed, so it's important to keep your dictator hat on the shelf and let your teen contribute to the outcome. Calmly talk about their mistake to figure out what to do not to repeat the same mistake. Shift your thinking from "How do I fix things?" to **"How do I enable my teen to fix things and come up with solutions for themselves?"** Showing them respect and the value of creative solutions will serve them greatly in the future.

> *We use this approach on a daily basis in our teaching environments. The impact is incredibly positive as children are given the chance to take ownership of their issues and solutions. When our students come to us with a problem, we generally approach it by asking, "What is the underlying problem?" "How can I help or support you with this?" "What could you do or change to try to resolve the issue?" "Is there anything we can work on together to improve the situation?" In fact, this is a strategy we often recommend to parents, and we always receive impressive feedback on how well this works.*

Write things down. In any relationship, and especially during conflict, it's important to try to understand the other side. Likewise, we also need to feel understood. Not everyone feels eloquent under stress, and it can be difficult to find the correct words to express exactly what you mean. Sometimes the best way to do so is in writing. Carefully writing down your emotions, hurts and expectations not only makes things clearer in your own mind; the other person is also able to re-read the information and process it properly in their own time. Letters help avoid miscommunication and further misunderstandings.

If all else fails, try mediation. Sometimes we all need external help, and that's where witnesses and mediators come in. Mediation involves having a neutral third party, either a trusted family friend or a professional, who is willing and able to manage the conflict in a confidential, constructive manner. Mediators don't necessarily take sides, give advice or offer solutions, but instead maintain a safe, balanced and focused space for practical and positive solutions to be found. This type of environment can be extremely useful for recurring conflicts, highly emotional parents or teens, and in situations where resolution seems hopeless.

Benefits of Parent-Teen Conflict

No one particularly likes conflict, but think about it this way: If your teens were always compliant and agreed with everything you told them, chances are they would become adults that are very passive and easily taken advantage of. We all want our children to be able to stand up for themselves, don't we?

Conflict helps shape our adult relationship with our child, and although we need to be strong in our role as the parent, we also have to allow for the discussion to take a more peer-to-peer dynamic. During arguments, teens are testing their growing self-reliance and experimenting with their newfound adult logic and reason. Who else are they going to practice on?

In an article entitled Development of Parent–Adolescent Relationships: Conflict Interactions as a Mechanism of Change published in *Child Development Perspectives*, Susan Branje explains that conflicts are essential for the long-term health of the evolving parent-child relationship. It's during conflict that the relationship grows to a more level playing field, where one participant is no longer necessarily better or stronger than the other. As parents let go of control and teens step into adulthood, there tends to be less conflict. It has been replaced by a more balanced peer-to-peer connection.

Susan Branje's study also shows that parents and children with a generally good relationship deal with conflict better, whereas more fragile families have a harder transition into adulthood and tend to grow apart at this time. In fact, teenagers who are raised in families who argue a lot are more likely to have lower self-esteem and more behavioural issues. This can generate a vicious cycle of more conflict, potential substance abuse, negative internalization and acting out, which in turn can lead to more conflict, and so on.

It's never too late to create a loving and supportive family environment, where adolescents can learn to handle conflict safely. Soon, there will likely be plenty of opportunities for them to test their resilience, convictions and conflict resolution skills outside the home!

Although grueling at the time, conflict offers first-hand experience on how to win and lose a battle. It teaches assertiveness, confidence, and self-trust — all qualities that develop character and inner strength.

We all need to take responsibility for our actions and own our mistakes. It may seem like a roundabout way to get there, but parent-teen conflict is, in fact, a brilliant way for your relationship to evolve. And of course, this is easier if both parents are on the same page.

Finally, set realistic consequences that you are able to keep yourself. Why make it worse for yourself by giving punishments or repercussions that will also be painful for you? We'll look at some of the best natural and controlled types of consequences next.

SEVEN

THE POWER OF NATURAL AND CONTROLLED CONSEQUENCES

Consequences are always a hot topic with parents, debatable depending on the severity of the 'crime' and all the corresponding circumstances. No matter how many years of practice we have, we never seem to be quite sure if the consequences of our child's actions are appropriate, too strict, or not enough. This is especially true when it comes to controlled consequences, meaning the ones that we, ourselves, decide and impose on our children. They're the rewards and punishments that we give them based on their decisions, behaviours and actions.

It's important to realize that punishment is never the goal with our children. According to parenting expert Amy McCready, punishment is often associated with pain, blame or shame. We're forcing our teens into submission by overpowering them with fear, which causes them to shut down. This strategy can be harmful and is not at all conducive to personal growth. What's more, most children who are punished a lot also tend to become very good at lying in order to avoid the harsh consequences.

Positive discipline, on the other hand, reinforces consequences that provide a life lesson our sons and daughters can learn from. Through their mistakes, they should be gaining an insight into how the world works, how their choices affect others, what is acceptable and what isn't.

One of the best ways to experience the world is through natural consequences, which are the logical outcomes of the decisions we make. If we go to bed too late, we won't perform as well the next day. If we take our anger out or are rude to our friends, they may feel hurt and not want to talk to us for a while. If we get caught cheating or lying, others might decide not to trust us anymore.

Through trial and error, these are lessons we've all learned as adults, not because they were imposed on us, but because they are universal truths and we often had to learn them the hard way. That's the beauty of natural consequences — there's no input needed from us. All we have to do is sit back and watch nature take its course.

Allowing Natural Consequences to Flow

Natural consequences reinforce the reasons we instilled the rules in the first place — and the best part is that we don't have to do the correction ourselves.

There comes a point when we need to step aside and allow our teens to learn life lessons for themselves. That's not easy to do — we've spent the last decade, and more, wrapped up in trying to control all the details of our children's lives. As they approach adulthood, we need to empower them to take control of their own lives.

Think about it: We learn best from doing things hands-on, from being out there, practicing and making mistakes. Often the best way to learn is the hard way.

Not only does this process build resilience in teens, but it helps them think about the potential consequences of their behaviour. Instead of simply acting on their instincts, they have to begin evaluating the weight of their actions. "Is what I'm about to do right? And is it worth it?"

Natural consequences call on our teen's problem-solving skills, and give them a taste of real life as an adult, without having their parents in the background controlling the outcomes. As a result of this, these types of consequences also help us avoid the frustrating power struggles we can so easily get into with our teens. Instead of arguing with your 15-year-old daughter to put on a longer skirt and warmer footwear in the winter, what would happen if we just let her get cold? How long would it take for her to feel enough discomfort to realize on her own that life is better with boots on?

Kate became exasperated with continuously nagging her son to study for his sophomore year exams. He didn't do as well as he thought he might have and was very disappointed in himself. Kate found that when he entered his junior year, he

had his head down and became self-driven. He
had learned the lesson for himself.

Allowing natural consequences to take place requires us to consciously hold ourselves back and not intervene. Instead, try going with the flow. The most rewarding part of allowing natural consequences to teach your teen is that you don't have to come up with anything yourself. Instead, you're simply trusting the universe to determine the outcomes that certain choices lead to. These outcomes can come from outside forces and authority figures, like teachers or police, yet they can also come from you setting limits on how much you will do for your child.

Of course we're here to protect them, but there are certain cases in which we should let nature take the lead.

1. **Responsibility for their belongings.** By adolescence, they should know how to take care of their things. It's no longer up to us to make sure they have everything they need before leaving the house, or that they lock up their bicycle so it doesn't get stolen. If they forget their books at home, for instance, they'll have to learn to share with a classmate or deal with the teacher's discipline. If they leave their dirty clothes on their bedroom floor and run out of clean clothes to wear, eventually they'll have to learn to do their own laundry. If they carelessly break their new smartphone, they'll have to live without one for a

while, or until they can save up their money for a
new one.

2. **Their behaviour at school.** No parent likes
   to hear that their child failed a test or got
   detention for being rude to the teacher. If your
   teen doesn't do their homework, however, they'll
   have to deal with a bad grade, or having to stay
   behind to catch up. In the real world, this is what
   happens when you don't take your
   responsibilities seriously. It's the same as far as
   bad behaviour goes. Don't forget that the story
   your teen tells you is only one side of what
   happened. There are many more angles that we
   don't know about simply because we're not there,
   and that's okay. Children make mistakes, and
   teachers know this all too well. That's why we
   should allow teachers to take charge of the
   consequences of wrongdoings at school. Not only
   does this leave us out of the mix, but it reinforces
   to our teens that we're not going to bail them out
   all the time.

On the other hand, there's no need to add any more consequences at home for what has already been dished out at
school. If you feel like the school is dealing with things
appropriately, then allow them to do so. You don't want to
undermine their authority.

1. **Household chores.** Teens often get rewarded
   for participating around the house, whether that
   be with an allowance or extra privileges. When
   their chores don't get done on time, however,
   they'll have to deal with the consequences,

meaning that either they don't get paid or that they have to make it up with other chores. For this to work, we have to establish the rules in advance and make sure they're clear to everyone.

2. **Acting out in the real world.** If it doesn't pose a safety risk or have a major implication on how your teen is seen in the eyes of others, then allow your child to behave how they believe they should. If they're being loud and disrespectful, they'll learn from their neighbours, or whoever's around, that this is inappropriate behaviour. If they get a parking ticket or speeding fine, they'll quickly learn the price of not following the law.

If your son goes to bed too late because he has been too busy partying and drinking, gaming or snapchatting, for example, it's only natural that he'll be tired the next day. This may lead to forgetfulness, lower performance, getting worn out and catching a cold before the big event...

There's so much to learn from difficult situations, disappointment, discomfort, failure. The hardest part as a parent is trying not to 'rescue' our teens when something doesn't go the way they'd planned.

We learned this the hard way ourselves when we rescued our teens many times by going the extra mile just to ensure they had everything they required for their school lessons — from driving all the way back home just to collect a guitar and mouthguard for rugby to heading back halfway down the journey to school to collect an apron for a food technology lesson. With patterns like this repeating far too often, we made the decision to just let things take their natural course and teach our children to be more organized through natural consequences. It was only when we started using this approach that we noticed our children becoming more responsible and better organized.

Still, we have to learn to say: "This isn't my problem. You're the one who made the decision to act this way, and this is the consequence for that. What are you going to do differently next time?"

When Not to Use Natural Consequences

Of course, if it's dangerously cold outside and the consequences of wearing a mini-skirt could become a health or safety hazard, then we need to step in. We have to use good judgment and not necessarily let our teens try something dangerous just so they can learn from the natural consequences. Remember, as parents, our children expect us to intervene when it comes to safety. And so we should.

This is true when their own safety or the safety of others is at stake. You'd never, for example, allow your teens to experiment with drinking and driving. The natural consequences of this could be lethal. You may, however, try to teach them about responsible consumption by allowing them to have a few drinks with you at home.

We should also intervene when the outcomes of their actions are delayed and things can spiral out of hand, like the consequences of not taking care of their health, for example, or developing generally bad habits that could affect their grades, or their future. When their negative behaviour affects their long-term health and wellbeing, it's time for us to step in with more controlled consequences.

Applying Effective Controlled Consequences

Teens are not as malleable or as easily influenced by us as they were when they were younger, so it may take more work for them to change their negative patterns and behaviours — much like it's a huge effort for us to change the way we interact with our teens. Still, with patience comes hope. And with patience, we may be able to come up with consequences that will lead our teens to grow from these lessons.

When it comes to discipline, and with almost everything regarding our children, in fact, we have to be consistent in our love, our words and our actions. Because they can't always put their exact thoughts and emotions into words, we have to listen very carefully to them, beyond what they're telling us, and observe them so that we get to know them on a more intimate level. What motivates them? What type of consequence would affect them the most? How do they learn best? Each family is different, so we have to be creative.

Effective consequences should teach our teens how to change their bad behaviours. As James Lehman, founder of Empowering Parents.com said, "You can't punish kids into acceptable behaviour." And he was right. Lehman suggests that we sit down with our teens and agree on the privileges and consequences of misbehaviour together.

Remember that for a lesson to work well, the privilege we're taking away should be one that our child will actually miss. Lehman encourages us not to give in, and to withhold that privilege until our teen has successfully experienced or completed their consequence. By defining the consequences beforehand, our teens know what to expect and we, as parents, are better equipped to react in the heat of the moment.

Here are some solid guidelines borrowed in part from Lehman's Total Transformation Program that will help you set effective consequences.

1. **Consequences must be related to your teen's original behaviour.** If your teen is late for curfew, for instance, then you should make them come home earlier the next two or three times they go out.

2. **Consequences must be respectful to your teen.** The rules have to be established beforehand and the consequences need to have been made clear to them before they went out and broke the rules. To make sure they understand these consequences clearly, have your teen repeat them to you when you establish them together. This is considered playing fair, and

proof that everyone involved understands what's at stake.

3. **They must be reasonable.** How badly did your teen break the rules? Does it warrant being grounded for one day, one week, or one month? What's the best way for them to learn their lesson then be allowed to go back out into the world to try again?

If after the defined period of time your teen didn't manage to learn the lesson you were hoping they would, there's no point in stretching the punishment out any longer. This probably won't help and will just demotivate everyone involved. We don't always get things right either, so instead, let's just try to think of a better way to teach our lesson the next time.

Controlled Consequences That Work

Here are some of the consequences we have found to be effective, though our teens tend to disagree and not like them quite so much!

Take away their electronic devices. This is probably the one consequence that will affect today's connected teens the most. But you may actually notice an improvement in your teen's attitude after a period of tech-detox and adaptation. Get ready for lots of nagging and empty promises on their end with this punishment, but remember to be consistent with your decision.

Don't threaten something and not follow through with it. This method of restricting privileges also works with other cherished items or activities. You wouldn't want to stop them from participating in their favourite after-school activity, but you may want to restrict access to the car, or not give them pizza money for the week.

Assign extra physical work. Not only is physical labour healthy and helps them sweat out some of their extra energy and frustrations, but it also comes with the satisfaction of seeing actual progress after a job. This can boost their morale, and they may even begin to enjoy it! Assigning extra chores is also a good way to make them think twice about their behaviour the next time.

Money talks. Money is a great motivator, and it can be used as a reward for a job well done. It can also be taken away, or reduced, as a consequence of bad behaviour or not having completed their chores, for example.

Just walk away. Some people thrive on conflict and argument, which is why they seek it out on a regular basis. If you find that this is the case with your son or daughter, just stay calm and tell them that you'll continue the discussion once they've cooled down. There's nothing worse than not having anyone to argue with when you're in the mood for a fight. The same goes for other mild misbehaviour that's not harmful to anyone or anything, like leaving a mess in the kitchen or speaking in a grumpy tone. If we don't give the situation any energy to grow, chances are it will go away.

Help them make up for their mistakes. If your teen's choices hurt someone or damaged any property, then they should deal with the direct consequences of their actions. For instance, if they borrow something without asking then break or lose it, they'll have to fix it or pay for it. Making amends with sincere apologies to those affected is also a valuable way for our teens to feel a bit of personal shame and own up to their mistakes.

Regaining Privileges

Most of our consequences or punishments come with time restrictions. For example, we'll decide to take away our teen's phone for two days, or reduce curfew by one hour for two weeks.

Another tactic is to have our teens earn back their privileges. So if we find that they're sneaking on the lights after bedtime, not sleeping enough and getting up late, maybe we can take away their phone every day after 8 pm until they show us that they're able to be ready on time in the mornings.

When one of Liz's teens was not getting on with the

reading or studying schedule they had agreed on,
she missed out on her next outings with friends
in order to use the time to catch up.

Finally, we'd all like to experience more fun, lighthearted moments with our teens than heavy, negative ones, which is why we should try to focus on positive expectations rather than punishment. Be proactive in finding ways for them to express themselves and shine, and guide them to try out new things. If they feel positively challenged and stimulated, they are more likely to feel good about themselves and stay away from trouble.

Design an Agreement That Works

As we've seen throughout this book, it's best to get our teens involved in important family decisions. That, of course, means getting their input on how they see themselves evolving in the future. As they grow up and seek more independence, we should recognize this and help guide them through the process and assume the right amount of responsibility for their age.

Teen behaviour expert Josh Shipp suggests we create a contract with our teens outlining privileges, expectations and consequences. Now, as parents, the only thing we're truly required to provide for our children is food, shelter and safety. Anything else is considered a privilege, and it's important for our teens to realize the part we play in their freedom and wellbeing — and, for the most part, just how lucky they are.

Privileges. To begin, ask your teen to list the freedoms and privileges they'd like to experience at that time. This could be anything from having access to their mobile phones to special activities and having the right to go on outings with their friends. Some families renew these contracts every three to six months, just to keep up with their teen's ever-changing tastes and capabilities. Be as generous as possible, and if their requests are age-appropriate and not dangerous, then list them on the contract.

Expectations. Next, it's time for us, as parents, to list all the expectations we have concerning our teens. This may include showing respect for others, making efforts when it comes to school and activities as well as communicating openly about any issues they may have. This should also include all of the details related to each expectation, as well as the list of household chores you've both decided on. Don't forget to state any non-negotiables here, items like missing important family events, lying, or drinking and driving. Be as specific as possible so there's no way for anyone to misinterpret this part of the deal.

Another valuable point to include in this section is a code-word strategy that you and your teen can decide on together. All teens want to fit in, but what if they're put in a situation in which they're afraid or uncomfortable? Peer pressure becomes especially rampant in adolescence, so choosing a word or phrase that your son or daughter can use to get out of a challenging or risky situation can help them feel and stay safe without losing face in front of their peers.

How does this work? Instead of admitting their fears and discomfort to their friends, they can pretend that they have to call you to check in. Seemingly annoyed by your parental expectations, they can, in front of their peers, let you know they're in an awkward situation by using your code phrase, which could be something like, "Mom, I think I forgot to lock the back door," or "I'm staying out late tonight so I won't be able to visit Grandpa in the morning." This is your cue to pretend to get angry and make your teen come home right away. You end up being the bad guy in this case, which for a teenager is much better than admitting to their friends that they don't like the situation they're in.

Consequences. Finally, in the consequences section of your family agreement, clearly state what will happen if these expectations are not met. Make sure to use the guidelines listed above when deciding on appropriate consequences. That is, they need to be related to the original misbehaviour and be respectful and reasonable in both time and severity. In other words, certain privileges will be reduced, or removed, until the lesson has been learned.

Once you've all agreed on the three sections, everyone signs the contract to seal the deal.

By having this clear understanding written out beforehand, it eliminates any emotions or hard feelings you or your teen may have when consequences need to occur.

Your kids may still make a fuss — and really, who likes having their privileges taken away? When that happens, gently remind them that you all agreed on this together, that you're only upholding your part of the contract and you hope that, soon, they'll be able to do the same.

What's more, these types of clear, written family agreements give teenagers a sense of structure and security and may even bring your family closer. Everyone knows what the others want and expect in return. It's also a valuable opportunity to learn the give-and-take required to navigate real-life adult relationships. The more you give, the more you get.

Josh Shipp provides a downloadable template on his website, so feel free to inspire yourself from his example.

Empowering Teens to Own Their Decisions

Now, it's all written down and everyone knows what to expect in terms of privileges and consequences. But wouldn't it be wonderful if, instead of having to coerce our children to behave in a certain way, they took responsibility themselves?

By flipping the coin and having their privileges become the rewards of their actions, they learn that positive behaviour leads to good things. In other words, instead of taking away privileges because of bad behaviour, we add privileges because of good behaviour.

This encourages them to learn and adopt the valuable concept of personal responsibility.

> *If I want to do some gaming or go out with my friends,* for example, *then I need to make sure that I've done my homework and spent some quality time with the family.*

Yet how many of our teens rush with their homework or chores just to be able to go out with their friends sooner? Everyone tries to get away with this, so the only way to ensure a certain standard of quality is to verify what our teens have done before they can enjoy their privileges. Until they've proven that they can be trusted to perform their tasks to the best of their abilities (nobody's asking them to be perfect!), then it's our responsibility as parents to check that yes, indeed, they have done work to a level they can be proud of. Instilling this feeling of pride in a job well done should inspire our teens in the long run. But remember: if we expect them to make the extra effort, we need to make the effort ourselves.

Help Your Teens Own Their Decisions

This same notion of personal responsibility can be applied when it comes to important decisions. As your child's ability to use logic and reasoning grows alongside their quest for independence, it's time to slowly hand over some of that responsibility. Here are some ways to encourage your teen to find solutions for their problems and this, all with a positive mindset.

Identify and focus. Ask your teen, "What's the real problem here, and what kind of outcome would you like to see?" By helping them identify and then focus on the issue rather than the person or emotion associated with it, they will be able to tackle it more coolly and confidently.

Brainstorm and evaluate solutions. How could this problem be solved? All ideas are good at this stage, so give your child the space to explore. Then, teach your teen how to establish the pros and cons of each option. Once that's done, dismiss the ones that have more negatives than positives, and narrow out the most promising solutions. Stand back — but don't go too far in case you're needed for some constructive advice.

Go for it! Encourage them to choose the best solution and implement their ideas to solve the problem. Try to just listen and observe as your teen works towards resolving their conflict. And if the outcome isn't what they'd hoped, that's okay. They've certainly acquired some valuable problem-solving skills in the process.

Disciplining is part of a parent's job, and although it should be taken seriously, try not to let your teen's mistakes and your own decisions weigh you down.

Be creative. Each family is different, so really observe what works best when disciplining your teens and guiding them towards better decisions. Being a conscious parent requires us to come up with solutions that will inspire our sons and daughters to grow in the right direction.

As James Lehman said, in order to be effective, a consequence needs to be short-term, task-specific and involve a privilege your child values. Our goal as parents is to raise teens who can deal with limits, set their own boundaries and take responsibility for their behaviour and decisions.

That said, don't spend too much time and energy focusing on their bad behaviour. Instead, try to really focus on the positive, and soon enough, you'll notice that this is being mirrored in their decisions.

In the next chapter, you'll find a long list of ways to bring lightheartedness and connection into your home. Ultimately, the underlying goal in our lives is to build positive short and long-term relationships between members of our households and to create fun, memorable moments that we can cherish and look back on with joy.

EIGHT

GAME-CHANGING WAYS TO GET YOUR TEEN TO VALUE YOUR FAMILY

"Families are the compass that guides us. They are the inspiration to reach great heights, and our comfort when we occasionally falter."

Brad Henry

L ooking back on the guidelines and strategies we've seen so far in this book, probably the most important is this: **your family is a team.** You're all on the same side — and if you're not, you should make that an urgent priority. Take pride in your family. Like teams, families are meant to progress together for the greater good of the group.

By this stage, our teens have learned the basics of life, and could probably survive on their own if they had to. Our parental objective now has switched to maintaining a positive relationship and providing healthy support as they prepare to eventually leave home.

It's vital to note that there is no such thing as a 'perfect family' and that all families have problems. If you are struggling with your teenager and are trying to do something about it, it means that you are attempting to improve your family relationships. And by having made it this far already, you're well on your way to a smoother home environment!

No matter what kind of family make-up we have and who's involved, be that siblings, grandparents or close friends, we should all be striving towards teamwork, cooperation and positive vibes within the home. This chapter gives us the game plan on how to achieve this.

Transform Your Family Into a Winning Team

The definition of a team is 'more than one person working together toward a common goal.' Sound familiar? As parents, we're the undisputable coaches of our own teams. Our objective is to build a strong bond in which the entire family feels safe and comfortable. Making sure that everyone is growing together can be a lot to juggle, especially when some of the team members are reluctant to play. That's why it's important to get everyone in the game now — and to keep practice time fun and lighthearted. Make sure the whole team is proud of their family.

You may have heard the expression, "There's no I in team." This motto promotes selflessness and cooperation. We learn to share when working together, and not only to think of ourselves but of others as well. As the leader, make sure that everyone helps others when they can, and that nobody feels left out. We all deserve to feel appreciated, loved and part of something bigger than ourselves. It feels good to know we'll always be there for each other, and our teens feel the same way.

Everyone's strengths and personality contribute to the family. It's important to recognize that even though we're all different individuals, we are able to work together towards a strong, happy home environment. Chances are we won't win all the challenges, but at least we'll have tried to surpass them together.

Now, let's look at the rule book for tips on transforming your family into a winning team. We have made a conscious plan to follow these tips in our daily lives and found a noticeable improvement in the way we work together with our families.

Share your skills. We all have talents we can bring to the table, and none is more important or valuable than the other. And of course, being part of a team is a prime opportunity to learn new skills as well. As adults, we have a lot to teach our children, but there are certainly some skills they are able to share with us, too, so be open to trying new things. Become a mentor to other team members if you can.

*In our households, we have found teaching new
skills like cooking, art, sports, sewing and
software use to be very valuable.*

Respect. Your teens should always feel included in the group, even during times of conflict and so-called despair. They play a major role in how the game is going, so it's important to focus on the positive and not just the hard times. Respect breeds respect, so make a point of reminding your kids how much they matter to you — and to the family team!

Have a common vision. Work towards a shared goal. Is there a project you'd all like to see happen? Something you're all planning and working towards together? Plan as a team and make sure everyone has a role in the outcome.

*In Liz's household, the home renovation project got
everyone involved and excited. Choosing colour
schemes, tiles, textures, wall coverings and
furniture for rooms was a valuable and
motivating joint project for the entire family.*

Practice clear and honest communication. This is what makes families flow. We may have to deal with difficult issues at times, but hopefully after integrating some of the strategies in this book you'll find it's easier to keep calm when discussing heavier topics. And if you're calm, you'll inspire calm for the others around you.

Open and truthful conversations are especially important during hard times. If we're not left to assume or wonder what the others are thinking, it makes it easier to overcome stress and not let the family team go down in a crisis. If we are able, and more importantly, willing to talk about everything, then we can feel reassured knowing we can surpass these difficult times together.

As our sons and daughters begin to branch out on their own, we can expect them to come home with some bad news at times. This often includes feelings of guilt or shame for having done something they may not be proud of. That's a perfectly normal part of growing up. Use some of the listening techniques we looked at in Chapter 4 to try to get your young adult to open up to you. And when they do, do not judge them. You're still part of the same team (there's no opting out of this one!), and that is true no matter how disappointed you may feel in the other person. Work towards a solution instead of holding grudges. Also, keep in mind that just because your teens don't share their mistakes openly, it doesn't mean they're not happening. Game plan aside, all winning coaches also rely on their gut instincts to better manoeuver their team.

Turn to trust. Trust is vital if any type of team is to function optimally. We all have to be honest, even when we feel it might hurt the other person. In fact, honesty should be one of the top items in the expectations section of the written agreement with your teen, which we saw in the previous chapter.

Apply your family's written agreement. Knowing who is responsible for what, as well as teen privileges and consequences, will keep expectations clearly marked in everyone's mind. We all feel stronger and more confident when we know what to anticipate.

Ways to Strengthen Your Family Bond

Accept your teens (and everyone else), for who they are, and don't try to change them. By now, our children have developed a sense of what they like and who they are trying to become, so allow your home to be the safe space they need to become that person. And remember, they are not you. They feel and react differently to situations, so as long as it's not disrespectful or dangerous to anyone, let them respond to situations in their own way. You are there to love them unconditionally and guide them towards the best version of themselves. Make sure home is a place where they feel accepted.

Stay calm, even when they're not. By not overreacting, they can feel safe knowing they can come to you for comfort and advice. Teens need us to be okay, especially when they're feeling at their most vulnerable and distraught. And although they may feel it's the end of the world, we need to show them that it's not.

Here are some ways to strengthen the family bond and have fun together.

Share meals together. We all have busy schedules, but try to have at least one meal a day as a family. Turn off the TV and leave phones in the other room. Do your best to make these moments fun and light — mealtimes are not the right time to impart heavy lessons. Prepare meals together whenever possible. There's always a job for everyone in the kitchen!

Create family traditions. Rituals give everyone on the team something to look forward to. Make sure you all set aside quality time and include it in your schedule. Family traditions could be something as simple as Monday movie nights, going out for pizza after school on Thursdays, or visiting Grandma for brunch every Sunday. Maybe there's that song you all sing along to together in the car on long trips. Of course your teen might be embarrassed by this, but it will definitely be something they'll remember for the rest of their lives.

Spend quality time together. Plan monthly family outings and give everyone a chance to select the activity. One-on-one time is also an important way to stay connected, so try to find alone time for each parent to spend with their teen. Teens can sometimes be selective when it comes to being seen out with their parents, so ask them to suggest an activity they'd like to do together. Movies, lunch, maybe a game... Find common interests despite your differences, and you'll soon observe this becoming a special treat for everyone.

Celebrate accomplishments. Take time to honour everyone's efforts and successes. This doesn't have to turn into a big celebration, but recognition of hard work and the right attitude make a big difference. Support your teen's hobbies. Also, make sure to acknowledge their failures and disappointments. Don't brush things under the rug. They may need to sit down and cry over a cup of tea, so be there for them with cookies and an open heart.

Schedule regular meetings. Whereas the activities mentioned above should be kept light and focused on nurturing positivity, these meetings can be used to discuss the more serious issues that occur naturally within all families and teams. Take this time to find solutions for problems. Make sure everyone has a chance to speak and be heard. And why not close these family meetings by ordering pizza?

By integrating these simple routines into your family, you create structure and help give your children something to be proud of.

Eight Fun Family Team-Building Activities

It's always a good idea to jump out of our comfort zones and do something a bit silly with our teens. After searching high and low for enjoyable team-building activities, we've narrowed it down to eight of our favourites. We recommend you try these with your families, too. We have used these and they've proven to be great fun no matter how old your kids are. Some of these activities require a bit of preparation, so why not get the whole family involved in that as well? Feel free to play with extended family members and friends — these are wonderful ways to keep the mood light and get everyone laughing. And why not have those with the lowest score prepare dinner together tonight?

1. **Home Trivia.** Divide your family into teams of two and ask them questions about their partner. "What is Dad's favourite dessert?" "What is Evie's favourite way to spend a Saturday?" "How many fish does Joe have in his aquarium, and what are their names?" Have each person write down the answers then check to see how well they know the other person.

2. Spin the Bottle. Play the sensible version where you spin the bottle and the person the top lands on must tell the truth about something. Or they could perform a challenge such as 20 press-ups, holding the plank for one minute or making everyone a cup of tea.

3. Drawing Challenge. Sit back-to-back with a partner. One person takes a pencil and a blank piece of paper, while the other person receives a piece of paper with a word on it like tree, apple or spider. The goal is for the person with the blank paper to recreate the drawing using only their partner's verbal instructions — but not the given word. So for tree, for example, they might say, "Draw two vertical lines in the middle of your paper which fan out at the top, then draw a cloud shape on top of the parts that fan out. Next, in the cloud shape, draw six little circles with a line coming out of the top centre of each one." Once you have finished giving instructions and your partner has finished the drawing, compare to see if you both have the same picture. This is great for practicing clear communication.

4. Kahoot Quiz - https://kahoot.com/ This is a quiz that can be found online. It is a fun quiz that is used in many learning environments at school but can be played at home with the family and friends. Set everyone up on their device or in pairs and decide on the topic for the quiz. Give yourselves quirky and fun names and play the quiz. This opens up a huge amount of excitement and discussion.

5. Water Relay. This is a great outdoor activity to do on a warm afternoon. Get a couple buckets of water and two empty water bottles. The objective is for both teams to fill their water bottle by passing down water from person to person using only the palms of their hands. You could also throw in some simple aids like spoons and straws. This challenge is guaranteed a laugh!

6. One-Handed Challenge. Get into pairs, then tie one person's left hand to the other person's right hand. Each couple then has to work together to accomplish some tasks with their free hand. These could include tying a shoelace, folding a towel, or putting a diaper on a doll. The sillier the better.

7. Make a Dessert. Get into pairs and have an array of ingredients to make a dessert. Set a time limit then get someone to give marks for taste and presentation.

8. Circuit Challenge. Exercising together creates bonding time that is filled with fun and laughter. This is a fantastic outdoor activity which can be done indoors, too. Set up five or six stations and mark them with cones or a beanbag. Next, label each station with an exercise activity such as: hold the plank, squats, jumping jacks, press-ups, sprinting on the spot, sit-ups and so on. One person keeps the time (one minute is usually good) and everyone starts doing their given exercise until the time is up. Then everyone rotates around to the next challenge and starts again.

Create a Positive Environment

In this final section, let's look at how to create an optimal home environment in which our teens can flourish. Home should always be a safe place for our kids to turn to. Those who grow up in a warm, loving home tend to have higher self-esteem, more developed communication skills and emotional intelligence that will help them thrive in all kinds of adult relationships outside of the family team.

Teens are sensitive creatures, but there are a few surefire ways that are bound to help them feel better about themselves. First of all, **physical activity is excellent for promoting a healthy body image,** especially when exercise is done outside the home in a gym or school setting.

And as anyone with teens knows, body insecurity can be a serious issue for many growing adolescents.

Don't compare your children to others, and try to explain to them that what they see on social media is not necessarily reality. Instead, **teach them to be gentle with themselves,** to listen to their bodies and appreciate what they have and who they are. They're not like the others, and that's wonderful! How boring would the world be if everyone was good at the same things? **Self-compassion, self-respect and self-care should be taught early on.** Once our teens learn healthy habits and feel comfortable with who they are, they'll be more likely to go out and share their compassion with the world.

Helping others is another way to help ourselves. How amazing does it feel to make someone smile? Teaching our teens to focus on those who need help is one of the most valuable lessons we can give them. Encourage them to volunteer in the community and to take part in projects that don't really concern them. Not only will this be beneficial to those on the receiving end, but it will open our teens up to new ideas and potential new passions.

And speaking of passions, make sure to **recognize your teen's strengths and celebrate their talents as much as possible.** Their interests and skill sets may not be the ones you had hoped they would be, but if they make your kids happy, then they deserve to be encouraged.

According to The Pragmatic Parent website, certain factors are more important than others in developing our teen's confidence and resilience.

Your words say it all. The voice you use when speaking to your child is the voice they hear in their heads. That's a load of pressure on us parents, but it also gives us a lot of power. We can choose to either encourage or discourage our sons and daughters. Which do you think will have a more positive short and long-term effect? That's right, so make sure to always choose kindness and encouragement.

Studies have shown that the tenderness or harshness of our words and feelings towards them are the basis of what our teens feel about themselves. While they are also influenced by their interactions with their peers, the core of their self-worth begins in the home. That's why love, patience, support and acceptance should always be present in your relationship — even when they've messed up, no matter how badly.

Show affection. Hug your teen and tell them you love them. This is especially true when they're hurt, or have done something wrong. These soft, physical gestures help reinforce your unconditional love. Some teens aren't very tactile, however, so make sure to respect that and only hug them if they want to be hugged.

Be a role model. They're observing everything we do, even when they're pretending to ignore us, and this includes the way we self-talk. This means that if they hear us being negative and talking down to ourselves, they'll do the same. If we're miserable, nagging and moody, that will rub off on them, too. They repeat what they see and hear from us, so make sure that you're behaving in a way that you'd like them to behave as well. Make an effort not to allow your bad habits to become their bad habits.

CONCLUSION - CONSCIOUS PARENTING, ONE STEP AT A TIME

Throughout this book, we've looked at ways to improve our relationship with our teenage sons and daughters. We've delved into how their brains work and develop over time, and how those changes influence their emotional and some-times irrational reactions. Now we understand more clearly why ideas that seem completely logical to us haven't even crossed their minds.

We've outlined the main parenting styles then reflected on how our own younger years impact the way we parent today. We've covered the most common issues that families with teenagers deal with, and given you strategies to communicate, negotiate and resolve conflict in a calmer, more conscious and confident manner.

Have you noticed your parenting style slowly evolving as you integrate some of the knowledge in this book? We certainly hope so!

It takes a special willingness and a great deal of effort to first recognize then acknowledge our weaknesses as individuals, and more specifically, as parents. It's even more challenging to finally begin to make the changes in ourselves that will allow us to grow into a better parent. But as you'll soon see, the improvement that this personal development brings to your relationship with your teen is well worth the effort.

Without realizing it, our positivity rubs off on others, so let's try to keep it on the forefront of everything we do in the home. Of course, certain moments and situations will be harder than others, but if we radiate love and acceptance, communicate kindly with others *and* ourselves, we're helping to build a family environment where everyone can learn and thrive, even in difficult times.

If your teen feels comfortable expressing themselves and sharing their feelings and ideas openly, without judgment, they will want to form a more positive relationship with the family. In turn, this means they would be more likely to consider and accept our parental guidance and perspectives on things. This cycle based on trust and respect should be the foundation on which we develop our values as conscious parents.

We've shared many tools here to help you in your transition to becoming a more conscious parent, but don't attempt to tackle them all at once. Integrate these new strategies one at a time, starting with whichever one feels easiest to you. Refer to chapters that are relevant to you at certain moments of your parenting journey and apply the strategies given. This will help you to build your foundation slowly, solidly and without stress.

Cultivate a growth mindset and nourish your connection with your teen. Make your home a safe and positive space, where it's okay to make mistakes because we know we always learn from these. And when you begin to notice that those little steps you have taken start to achieve greater success, you can reap the rewards of your ongoing patience, perseverance and commitment to your family.

"We had great faith that with patience, understanding, and education, my family and I could be helpful in changing minds and attitudes."

Ryan White

We would love to hear your feedback so that we can continue sharing our research and experiences with others just like you. We would be extremely grateful if you could leave a quick review on Amazon so that more parents can get the support they need. Together, we can all make a small difference in the hope that our children are leading happier and more prosperous lives today and in the future.

FURTHER READING

Kate Anderson and Liz Carrington

A Special Gift to Our Readers

Included with your purchase of this book is our '20 *Simple Tips You Must Use When Talking To Your Teen*' e-book.

This resource will prepare you with the best tools for communicating with your teens effectively and help build more positive relationships with them.

Click the link below or scan the QR code and let us know which email address to deliver it to.

http://eepurl.com/hESnOP

REFERENCES

In this section we have included a detailed list of references for each chapter in the book.

Chapter 1

Adolescent Emotional Development. (n.d.). Mental-help.Net. Retrieved October 18, 2021, from https://www.mentalhelp.net/adolescent-development/emotional/

AFG Guidance Center. (n.d.). *How Personality Develops & Changes in Teenagers.* AFG Family. Retrieved October 18, 2021, from https://afgfamily.com/blog/teens-2/personality-develop-teens/

Borghuis, J. (2017). *Big Five personality stability, change, and codevelopment across adolescence and early adulthood.*Psycnet.Apa. Retrieved October 18, 2021, from http://psycnet.apa.org/record/2017-09436-001

The Four Truths About What Teens Really Want. (2021, May 25). IMOM. Retrieved October 18, 2021, from https://www.imom.com/the-four-truths-about-what-teens-really-want/

Greenberg, B. (2017, March 10). *20 Reasons Why Your Teens Get Mad At You*. HuffPost. Retrieved October 18, 2021, from https://www.huffpost.com/entry/20-reasons-why-your-teens-get-mad-at-you_b_9402664#:%7E:text=1.,feel%20misunderstood%20by%20their%20parents.&text=They%20get%20mad%20when%20they,of%20think-ing%20that%20you%20do.

HealthyChildren.org - From the American Academy of Pedi-atrics. (n.d.). HealthyChildren.Org. Retrieved October 18, 2021, from https://www.healthychildren.org

Hudson, C. (2010a, May 19). *What Teenagers Think of Parents*. Understanding Teenagers. Retrieved October 18, 2021, from https://understandingteenagers.com.au/what-teenagersthinkofparents/

Hudson, C. (2010b, September 13). *Go With The Flow: 10 Ways to Easily Engage Teenagers*. Understanding Teenagers. Retrieved October 18, 2021, from https://understandingteenagers.com.au/go-with-the-flow-10-ways-to-easily-engage-teenagers/

Mental/Emotional/Social Changes through Puberty. (n.d.). Mentalhelp.Net. Retrieved October 18, 2021, from https://www.mentalhelp.net/parenting/mental-emotional-social-changes-through-puberty/

Raising Children AU. (2021, July 9). *Pre-teen and teenage development: what to expect*. Raising Children Network. Retrieved October 18, 2021, from https://raisingchildren.net.au/teens/development/understanding-your-teenager/teen-development#:%7E:text=Physical%20changes%20in%20teenagers&text=Physical%20changes%20in%

20puberty%
20include,of%20pubic%20and%20body%20hair

Wayne, J. (2015, June 3). *Why Your Teenager Gets So Annoyed With You*. HuffPost. Retrieved October 18, 2021, from https://www.huffpost.com/entry/why-your-teenager-gets-so-annoyed-with-you_b_6998688

Chapter 2

Bayless, K. (2019, December 6). *What Is Helicopter Parenting?* Parents. Retrieved October 18, 2021, from https://www.parents.com/parenting/better-parenting/what-is-helicopter-parenting/

Bright Horizons Education Team. (2021, September 16). *What Is My Parenting Style? Four Types of Parenting*. Bright Horizons. Retrieved October 18, 2021, from https://www.brighthorizons.com/family-resources/parenting-style-four-types-of-parenting

Campbell, L. (2016, May 23). *Free-Range Parenting: The Pros and Cons*. Healthline. Retrieved October 18, 2021, from https://www.healthline.com/health/parenting/free-range-parenting

Chaunie Brusie. (2017, June 22). *Should You Practice Permissive Parenting?* Healthline. Retrieved October 18, 2021, from https://www.healthline.com/health/parenting/what-is-permissive-parenting

Cherry, K. (2021a, April 29). *Are You a Permissive Parent?* Verywell Mind. Retrieved October 18, 2021, from https://www.verywellmind.com/what-is-permissive-parenting-2794957#:%7E:text=Permissive%20parenting%

2οis%2οa%
2οtype,friend%2οthan%2οa%2οparental%2οfigure.

Cherry, K. (2ο21b, July 26). *Uninvolved Parenting and Its Effects on Children.* Verywell Mind. Retrieved October 18, 2ο21, from https://www.verywellmind.com/what-is-uninvolved-parenting-2794958

Cherry, K. (2ο21c, October 11). *What Is Authoritarian Parenting?* Verywell Mind. Retrieved October 18, 2ο21, from https://www.verywellmind.com/what-is-authoritarian-parenting-2794955#:%7E:text= Authoritarian%2οparenting%2οis%2οa%2οparenting

Dewar, G. (2ο21, May 2ο). *The authoritarian parenting style: What does it look like?* PARENTING SCIENCE. Retrieved October 18, 2ο21, from http://parentingscience. com/authoritarian-parenting-style/

Family, T. A. (2ο11, August 3). *Attachment Parenting Our Teens | The Attached Family.* The Attached Family. Retrieved October 18, 2ο21, from http://theattachedfamily. com/membersonly/?p=2837#:%7E:text=Attachment% 2οParenting%2οmeans%2οallowing%2οyour,let-ting%2οgo%2οof%2οnurturing%2οthem.

Feuerman, M. (2ο19, November 11). *Saving Your Relationship When You Disagree on Parenting.* Verywell Family. Retrieved October 18, 2ο21, from https://www. verywellfamily.com/tips-dont-agree-on-parenting-41ο7372

Kuppens, S., & Ceulemans, E. (2ο19). *Parenting Styles: A Closer Look at a Well-Known Concept.* PubMed Central (PMC). Retrieved October 18, 2ο21, from https://www. ncbi.nlm.nih.gov/pmc/articles/PMC6323136/

Li, M. P. S. (2021, August 30). *Permissive Parenting – Why Indulgent Parenting Is Bad For Your Child*. Parenting For Brain. Retrieved October 18, 2021, from https://www.parentingforbrain.com/permissive-parenting/

Martin, P. (2005, February 23). *What kind of parent are you?* The Guardian. Retrieved October 18, 2021, from https://www.theguardian.com/lifeandstyle/2005/feb/23/familyandrelationships.children

McCready, A. (2021, February 4). *When Parents Disagree on Discipline: 8 Steps to Harmonious Parenting*. Positive Parenting Solutions. Retrieved October 18, 2021, from https://www.positiveparentingsolutions.com/discipline/parents-disagree-on-discipline

Morin, A. (2021a, September 27). *How Free-Range Parenting Can Benefit Your Child*. Verywell Family. Retrieved October 18, 2021, from https://www.verywellfamily.com/what-is-free-range-parenting-1095057

Morin, A. (2021b, October 9). *4 Types of Parenting Styles and Their Effects on Kids*. Verywell Family. Retrieved October 18, 2021, from https://www.verywellfamily.com/types-of-parenting-styles-1095045

Schremph, K., & Mommy, T. S. (2020, March 5). *Everything To Know About Uninvolved Parenting & The Effect It Can Have On A Child*. Scary Mommy. Retrieved October 18, 2021, from https://www.scarymommy.com/signs-uninvolved-parenting/

Winter, K. (2020, July 28). *How Attachment Parenting Works With Teens*. Conscious Parenting Revolution. Retrieved October 18, 2021, from https://www.consciousparentingrevolution.com/how-attachment-parenting-works-with-teens

Chapter 3

Corkhill, M. (2016, April 5). *How to parent with unconditional love - The Green Parent*. The Green Parent. Retrieved October 18, 2021, from https://thegreenparent.co.uk/articles/read/love-without-strings

Kazdin, A. C. R. (2009, January 27). *I Spy Daddy Giving Someone the Finger*. Slate Magazine. Retrieved October 18, 2021, from https://slate.com/human-interest/2009/01/your-kids-will-imitate-you-use-it-as-a-force-for-good.html

Kleimo, C. (2019a, May 22). *Answer These 15 Questions to Improve Your Parenting*. Sensory Mom. Retrieved October 18, 2021, from https://www.sensorymom.com/answer-these-15-questions-to-improve-your-parenting/

Kleimo, C. (2019b, May 22). *Answer These 15 Questions to Improve Your Parenting*. Sensory Mom. Retrieved October 18, 2021, from https://www.sensorymom.com/answer-these-15-questions-to-improve-your-parenting/

Morin, A. (2021, January 22). *How to Model the Behavior You Want Your Child to Exhibit*. Verywell Family. Retrieved October 18, 2021, from https://www.verywellfamily.com/role-model-the-behavior-you-want-to-see-from-your-kids-1094785

Parents: role models and positive influences for teenagers. (2019, January 25). Raising Children Network. Retrieved October 18, 2021, from https://raisingchildren.net.au/pre-teens/behaviour/encouraging-good-behaviour/being-a-role-model

Secrets to Unconditional Parenting. (n.d.). Teach Through Love. Retrieved October 18, 2021, from https://www.teach-through-love.com/unconditional-parenting.html#:%7E:text=Unconditional%20parents%20teach%20their%20children,well%2Dbeing%20of%20their%20children.&text=Parents%20are%20asked%20to%20take,to%20empathize%2C%20understand%20and%20connect

Sherkat, M. (2016, December 7). *How your parenting tactics influence your teen's problem behaviors: Discrepancy found between parents', teens' views of parenting style contributes to teens' behavior problems*. ScienceDaily. Retrieved October 18, 2021, from https://www.sciencedaily.com/releases/2016/12/161207184640.htm#:%7E:text=Using%20data%20from%20220%20families

Chapter 4

10 WAYS TO A BETTER RELATIONSHIP WITH YOUR TEENAGER. (n.d.). Families for Life. Retrieved October 18, 2021, from https://familiesforlife.sg/pages/Unavailable.aspx

Child Mind Institute. (2021, October 12). *Tips for Communicating With Your Teen*. Retrieved October 18, 2021, from https://childmind.org/article/tips-communicating-with-teen/

Communicating with Teenagers | SkillsYouNeed. (n.d.). Skills You Need. Retrieved October 18, 2021, from https://www.skillsyouneed.com/parent/communicating-with-teenagers.html

Edwards, G. (2012). *Deeper conversations with your teen: The questions you need to ask.* Focus on the Family. Retrieved October 18, 2021, from https://www.focusonthefamily.ca/content/deeper-conversations-with-your-teen-the-questions-you-need-to-ask

Fox, A. (2015, April 26). *10 Tips for Improving Parent-Teen Relationships.* HuffPost. Retrieved October 18, 2021, from https://www.huffpost.com/entry/10-tips-for-improving-parent-teen-relationships_b_6737916

Gavin, M. L. (2019, June). *Communication and Your 13- to 18-Year-Old (for Parents) - Nemours Kidshealth.* Nemours KidsHealth. Retrieved October 18, 2021, from https://kidshealth.org/en/parents/comm-13-to-18.html

Partnership to End Addiction. (2020, June 17). *How to Listen and Get Through to Your Teen.* Retrieved October 18, 2021, from https://drugfree.org/article/listen-teen/

Team, F. Z. (n.d.). *Can we talk? 100 questions your teen might actually answer.* Family Zone. Retrieved October 18, 2021, from https://www.familyzone.com/anz/families/blog/100-questions-for-teens

Tools for Listening to Your Teen. (2020, June 23). Focus on the Family. Retrieved October 18, 2021, from https://www.focusonthefamily.com/parenting/tools-for-listening-to-your-teen/

Wilson, J. (2018, June 8). *50 of the Best (and Fun!) Questions To Start a Conversation With Your Teen Boy.* Parent|re.Mix. Retrieved October 18, 2021, from https://www.parentremix.com/blog/2018/5/10/50-questions-moms-should-ask-teen-boys

Chapter 5

Abraham, K. L., Studaker-Cordner, M. L., K.L., & M.L. (2021, April 14). *Negotiating with Kids: When You Should and Shouldn't.* Empowering Parents. Retrieved October 18, 2021, from https://www.empoweringparents.com/article/negotiating-with-kids-when-you-should-and-shouldnt/

Branje, S. (2018, September 1). *Development of Parent–"Adolescent Relationships: Conflict Interactions as a Mechanism of Change.* Society for Research in Child Development. Retrieved October 18, 2021, from https://srcd.onlinelibrary.wiley.com/doi/full/10.1111/cdep.12278

Brill, A. (2018, March 12). *How To Discipline A Child That Breaks The Rules And Doesn't Listen.* Positive Parenting Connection. Retrieved October 18, 2021, from https://www.positiveparentingconnection.net/how-to-discipline-a-child-that-breaks-the-rules-and-doesnt-listen/

Devine, M. L., & M.L. (2021, May 6). *How To Talk To Teens | Talking to Teens.* Empowering Parents. Retrieved October 18, 2021, from https://www.empoweringparents.com/article/how-to-talk-to-teens-3-ways-to-get-your-teen-to-listen/

Encouraging Independence While Still Maintaining Boundaries With Teens. (2021, September 4). Verywell Family. Retrieved October 18, 2021, from https://www.verywellfamily.com/autonomy-definition-3288320#:%7E:text=Be%20sure%20to%20provide%20opportunities,or%20picking%20after%2Dschool%20activities.

Firestone, L. (2013, March 6). *Leaving Your Childhood Behind to Become a Better Parent.* Psychology Today.

Retrieved October 18, 2021, from https://www.psychologytoday.com/gb/blog/compassion-matters/201303/leaving-your-childhood-behind-become-better-parent

Focus on the Family. (2021, February 24). *Dealing With Lazy Teenagers*. Retrieved October 18, 2021, from https://www.focusonthefamily.com/family-qa/dealing-with-lazy-teenagers/

Guidance and Discipline for Skill Building for Your 17-Year-Old. (2021, May 18). Parenting Montana. Retrieved October 18, 2021, from https://parentingmontana.org/discipline-17/

Hamilton, S. (2020, December 3). *Teenager behaviour: 6 tips for dealing with moods, pushing boundaries and phone obsession.* HELLO! Retrieved October 18, 2021, from https://www.hellomagazine.com/healthandbeauty/mother-and-baby/20201203102006/teenage-behaviour-explained-by-therapist/

Healthy Families BC. (2014, November 30). *Dealing with Disrespectful Teenage Behaviour*. Retrieved October 18, 2021, from https://www.healthyfamiliesbc.ca/home/articles/dealing-disrespectful-behaviour-teens

Helping your Teen Develop Autonomy. (2019, January 28). Middle Earth. Retrieved October 18, 2021, from https://middleearthnj.org/2019/01/27/helping-your-teen-develop-autonomy/

Morin, A. (2021, August 30). *7 Ways to Deal With Disrespectful Back Talk From Your Teen.* Verywell Family. Retrieved October 18, 2021, from https://www.verywellfamily.com/disrespectful-back-talk-teen-2609130

Negotiating with pre-teens and teenagers. (2021, September 8). Raising Children Network. Retrieved October 18, 2021, from https://raisingchildren.net.au/teens/communicating-relationships/communicating/negotiating

Schartz, D. (2020, February 27). *7 Ways to Get Teenagers to Actually Listen to You.* Psychology Today. Retrieved October 18, 2021, from https://www.psychologytoday.com/gb/blog/adolescents-explained/202002/7-ways-get-teenagers-actually-listen-you

When and How to Negotiate with Your Kids. (2018, June 18). The Successful Parent. Retrieved October 18, 2021, from http://www.thesuccessfulparent.com

Wong, D. (2021, August 10). *Disrespectful Teenager? 10 Tips For Frustrated Parents.* Daniel Wong. Retrieved October 18, 2021, from https://www.daniel-wong.com/2018/03/19/disrespectful-teenager/

Wright, F., & F. (2019, February 4). *How to motivate a lazy teenager in 6 steps.* Bounty Parents. Retrieved October 18, 2021, from https://www.bountyparents.com.au/expert-advice/motivate-lazy-teenager/

Chapter 6

Blyth, B. (2006, March). *Parent – Teen Conflict, Managing it Constructively.* Mediate. Retrieved October 18, 2021, from https://www.mediate.com/articles/blythB1.cfm

Dealing With Addiction (for Teens) - Nemours Kidshealth. (n.d.). Kids Health. Retrieved October 18, 2021, from https://kidshealth.org/en/teens/addictions.html

Flannery, B. (2021, March 22). *Causes of Conflict Between Parents and Teenagers*. WeHaveKids. Retrieved October 18, 2021, from https://wehavekids.com/parenting/Sources-of-Conflict-Between-Parents-and-Teenagers#:%7E:text=Why%20Do%20Parents%20and%20Teens

Mather, B. (2017, November 6). *Breaking the Cycle: 8 Strategies for Dealing with Conflict with Your Young Teen*. Parenthetical. Retrieved October 18, 2021, from https://parenthetical.wisc.edu/2017/11/06/breaking-the-cycle-8-strategies-for-dealing-with-conflict-with-your-young-teen/

Research Digest. (2016, February 2). *Scientific evidence that counting to 10 helps control anger (sometimes)*. Retrieved October 18, 2021, from https://digest.bps.org.uk/2016/02/02/scientific-evidence-that-counting-to-10-helps-control-anger-sometimes/

Rethinking Parent-Teen Conflict. (2018, February 1). The Swaddle. https://theswaddle.com/rethinking-parent-teen-conflict/

Sanford, T. L. (2009, January 1). *Why Parents Want to Control Their Teens*. Focus on the Family. Retrieved October 18, 2021, from https://www.focusonthefamily.com/parenting/why-parents-want-to-control-their-teens/

Chapter 7

Appropriate Consequences for a Teen's Bad Behavior. (2014, January 13). Middle Earth. Retrieved October 18, 2021, from https://middleearthnj.org/2014/01/13/appropriate-consequences-for-a-teens-bad-behavior/

Brown, N. D. (2018, March 7). *Time to Switch from Consequences to Privileges*. Neil D. Brown, LCSW. Retrieved October 18, 2021, from https://neildbrown.com/17-blog/podcast/time-to-switch-from-consequences-to-privileges/

Devine, M. L., & M.L. (2021, July 2). *Effective Consequences for Teenagers* Empowering Parents. Retrieved October 18, 2021, from https://www.empoweringparents.com/article/why-dont-consequences-work-for-my-teen-heres-whyand-how-to-fix-it/

Ginsburg, K. (2019, October 28). *Blame Parents with a Code Word*. Center for Parent and Teen Communication. Retrieved October 18, 2021, from https://parentandteen.com/blame-parents-a-code-word-strategy/

Ginsburg, K. (2021, September 30). *Create a Teen Behavior Contract*. Center for Parent and Teen Communication. Retrieved October 18, 2021, from https://parentandteen.com/discipline-adolescent-responsibility-contract/

A Mom's Best List of Consequences for Teenagers. (2019, April 3). The Reluctant Cowgirl. Retrieved October 18, 2021, from https://thereluctantcowgirl.com/list-of-consequences-for-teenagers/

Morin, A. (2019, September 12). *How to Make Natural Consequences an Effective Discipline Tool*. Verywell Family. Retrieved October 18, 2021, from https://www.verywellfamily.com/natural-consequences-as-a-discipline-strategy-1094849

Rubino, M., PhD. (2018, September 22). *How Parents Can Use Natural Consequences with Teenagers*. Pleasant Hill, CA Patch. Retrieved October 18, 2021, from https://patch.com/california/pleasanthill/how-parents-can-use-natural-consequences-teenagers

Shameer, M. (2015, February 6). *https://search.google.com/structured-data/testing-tool/326769.* MomJunction. Retrieved October 18, 2021, from https://www.momjunction.com/articles/help-your-teen-solve-her-problems_00326769/

Shipp, J. (2014, October 13). *Parent and Teen Family Contract - parenting teenagers.* Josh Shipp: Education Speaker One Caring Adult. Retrieved October 18, 2021, from https://joshshipp.com/parent-teen-contract-parenting-teenagers/

Time to Switch from Consequences to Privileges. (2021, May 26). Neil D. Brown, LCSW. https://neildbrown.com/17-blog/podcast/time-to-switch-from-consequences-to-privileges/

Top Education Speaker Josh Shipp. (2013, July 8). *Setting Rules with your Teen* [Video]. YouTube. https://www.youtube.com/watch?v=HwWroUgdBag

Whyte, A. (2019, May 23). *Natural Consequences for Teens.* Evolve Treatment Centers. Retrieved October 18, 2021, from https://evolvetreatment.com/blog/natural-consequences-for-teens/

Chapter 8

Benjamin, A. E. (2019, May 29). *The Importance of Family Teamwork.* MetroFamily Magazine. Retrieved October 18, 2021, from https://www.metrofamilymagazine.com/the-importance-of-family-teamwork/

David, J. (2021, October 18). *30 Team Building Activities for Teens, Families and Couples.* Sign Up Genius. Retrieved October 18, 2021, from https://www.signupgenius.com/home/team-building-activities-teens-families-couples.cfm

Dungy, L. (2021, February 25). *3 Ways to Make Your Family a Team.* IMOM. Retrieved October 18, 2021, from https://www.imom.com/3-ways-make-family-team/

Eva, A. L. (2018, May 21). *Five Ways to Help Teens Feel Good about Themselves.* Greater Good. Retrieved October 18, 2021, from https://greatergood.berkeley.edu/article/item/five_ways_to_help_teens_feel_good_about_themselves

Garrity, A., & Lascala, M. (2021, September 7). *45 Family Quotes to Remind You How Strong Those Bonds Are.* Good Housekeeping. Retrieved October 18, 2021, from https://www.goodhousekeeping.com/life/parenting/g25412857/family-quotes/

Help Your Teen Now. (2017, January 18). *10 Team Building Activities To Do With Your Family.* Retrieved October 18, 2021, from https://helpyourteennow.com/10-team-building-activities-to-do-with-your-family/

Norman, R. (2020, June 10). *How to Create a Family Your Kids Are Proud Of.* A Mother Far from Home. Retrieved October 18, 2021, from https://amotherfarfromhome.com/how-to-create-a-family-the-kids-want-to-come-home-to/

Relationships with parents and families: pre-teens and teenagers. (2021, September 14). Raising Children Network. Retrieved October 18, 2021, from https://raisingchildren.net.au/teens/family-life/family-relationships/relationships-with-parents-teens

Schlagheck, K. (2019, November 20). *Creating a Winning Family Team*. Live Smart Ohio. Retrieved October 18, 2021, from https://livesmartohio.osu.edu/family-and-relationships/schlagheck-110su-edu/creating-a-winning-family-team/

Set the Tone for a Happy Home: Create a Positive Home for your Kids. (2020, August 4). The Pragmatic Parent. Retrieved October 18, 2021, from https://www.thepragmaticparent.com/positivehome/

Printed in Great Britain
by Amazon

75172987R00111